REFORMING
PROBATION AND PAROLE

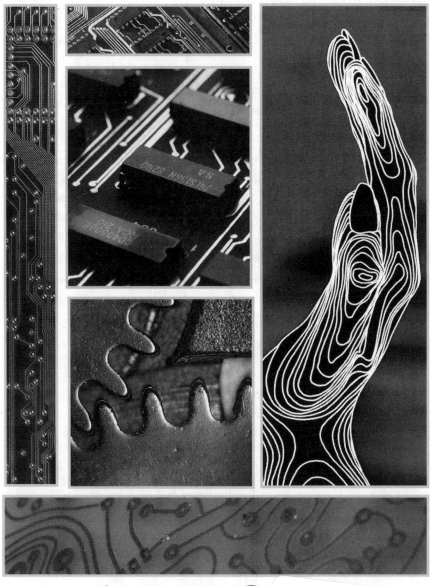

— In the 21st Ce

JOAN PETERSILIA,

Printed in the United States of America by Graphic Communications, Inc.,
    Upper Marlboro, Maryland.

For information on publications and videos available from ACA, contact our worldwide web home page at: http://www.corrections.com/aca or www.aca.org

ISBN 1-56991-144-4

This publication may be ordered from:
American Correctional Association
4380 Forbes Boulevard
Lanham, Maryland 20706-4322
1-800-222-5646

Library of Congress Cataloging-in-Publication Data

Petersilia, Joan.
        Reforming probation and parole / Joan Petersilia.
            p. cm.
        Includes bibliographical references.
        ISBN 1-56991-144-4 (pbk.)
        1. Probation–United States. 2. Parole–United States. I. Title.
        HV9304 .P462001
        364.6'2'0973–dc21   2001034324

Dedication

For my sons, Jeffrey and Kyle, who came from heaven to show me the most beautiful things in life.

—Joan Petersilia

Contents

Foreword

These essays explain the basic issues and trends in probation and parole today, and I believe they provide an excellent overview of this area of criminal justice for students as well as professionals. The questions at the end of each chapter enable readers to review the main concepts and test their knowledge of what they have read.

Dr. Petersilia points out that fewer resources are expended in probation and parole than in other facets of criminal justice and corrections. With her call for reform, she essentially asks policy makers: Is this is a cost-effective stratagem? If 2 percent of U.S. adults are on probation, then keeping them out of prison is a worthy goal for all of society. This goal is not feasible with probation officers shouldering triple digit caseloads. Likewise, discretionary parole release and parole field services have undergone major changes as the nation has embraced more punitive policies. Many states have eliminated parole release completely or severely limit its use. Parole supervision remains, but needed treatment programs are scarce, and many parole agencies focus on surveillance more than rehabilitation.

The focus of these essays is adult corrections. However, Dr. Petersilia's ideas about progressive parole—including community policing and supervision/treatment models that are not one-size-fits-all—could be used by forward-thinking juvenile corrections professionals in their research and practice.

These essays provide the groundwork for a solid discussion about what is needed to reform probation and parole. I hope that they will be read widely by policy makers, practitioners, and students in criminal justice and social science education programs.

James A. Gondles, Jr., CAE
Executive Director
American Correctional Association

PART ONE

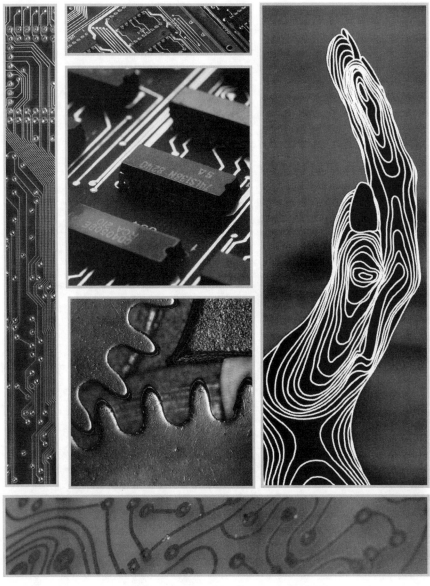

PROBATION AND
INTERMEDIATE SANCTIONS
IN THE UNITED STATES

CHAPTER ONE

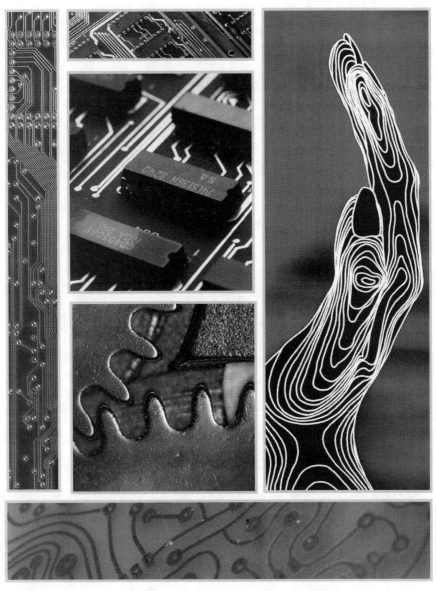

Probation and Intermediate Sanctions in
the United States: An Introduction[1]

The Popularity of Probation

Probation is the most common form of criminal sentencing in the United States. The American Correctional Association (1998) defines it as:

> A court-ordered disposition alternative through which an adjudicated offender is placed under the control, supervision, and care of a probation staff member in lieu of imprisonment, so long as the probationer meets certain standards of contact.

The Bureau of Justice Statistics (2000b) reports that nearly 4 million adults were under state or federal probation at year end 1999, and that probationers make up 60 percent of all adults under correctional supervision. In fact, the number of persons on probation is so large that the U.S. Department of Justice estimates that, on any one day, nearly 2 percent of all U.S. adult citizens are under probation supervision. And the probation population continues to rise—increasing more than 40 percent since 1990 (Bureau of Justice Statistics, 2000b).

Despite its wide use, probation is often the subject of intense criticism. It suffers from a "soft on crime" image, and as a result, maintains little public support. Probation often is depicted as permissive, uncaring about crime victims, and blindly advocating a rehabilitative ideal while ignoring the reality of violent, predatory criminals.

This poor (and some believe, misunderstood) public image leaves probation officials unable to compete effectively for scarce public funds. Nationally, community corrections receives less than 10 percent of state and local government

---

[1]This section has been updated and revised from "Probation in the United States" by Joan Petersilia, originally published by the University of Chicago in *Crime and Justice: A Review of Research*, Volume 22, 1997.

expenditures for corrections, even though probation agents supervise two out of three correctional clients (Petersilia, 1995b).

Reinventing Probation

As a result of inadequate funding, probation often means freedom from supervision. Offenders in large urban areas often are assigned to a probation officer's hundred-plus caseload, where meetings occur, at most, once a month, and there is little monitoring of employment or treatment progress. As long as no rearrest occurs, offenders can successfully complete their probation whether or not they have met their conditions fully or paid their court fees (Langan, 1994). Such "supervision" not only makes a mockery of the justice system, but leaves many serious offenders unsupervised.

But while current programs often are seen as inadequate, the concept of probation has a great deal of appeal. As Burton Roberts, administrative judge of the Bronx Supreme and Criminal Courts explained: "Nothing is wrong with probation. It is the execution of probation that is wrong" (cited in Klein, 1997:72).

Scholars and citizens agree that probation has many advantages over imprisonment, including lower cost, increased opportunities for rehabilitation, and reduced risk of criminal socialization. And along with prison crowding, probation is a nationwide problem. The need for inexpensive and flexible community punishment options has never been greater. Probation leaders (Reinventing Probation Council, 1999), policy makers (Bell and Bennett, 1996), and scholars (Clear and Braga, 1995; Smith and Dickey, 1998; Petersilia, 1998) are now calling for "reforming," "reinvesting," and "restructuring" probation.

Drug Courts

But exactly how would one go about reforming probation? Some are beginning to offer suggestions. There is a general trend toward greater judicial involvement in monitoring probation conditions. In many jurisdictions, judges have established special drug courts. More than 400 drug courts exist nationwide with some in most of the 50 states and the District of Columbia (Gebelein, 2000).

Here, judges identify first-time drug offenders, sentence them to participate in drug testing and rehabilitation programs, and then the judge personally monitors their progress. If the offender successfully completes the program, he or she is not incarcerated and in some jurisdictions (for example, Denver, Colorado), the conviction is expunged from the official record.

Research on drug courts has been limited, but some early studies have shown reductions in recidivism (Goldkamp, 1994) and increased offender participation in treatment (Deschenes, Turner, and Greenwood, 1995). After 1999, Delaware drug courts reported that 2,670 entrants—almost 50 percent—graduated their programs and had their charges dropped. Treatment providers attest that their drug court clients are more likely than other clients to finish treatment (Gebelein, 2000). One review of drug courts by Columbia University's Center on Addiction and Substance Abuse found reduced recidivism over months (or years) among drug-court participants (Belenko, 1998).

Other judges have decided on an individual basis to impose probation sentences that are more punitive and meaningful. A judge in Houston, Texas, forced a sixty-six-year-old music instructor who had molested two students to give up his $12,000 piano and post a sign on his front door warning children to stay away. State District Judge Ted Poe also barred the teacher from buying another piano, and even from playing one until the end of his twenty-year probation term (Mulholland, 1994).

But meting out individualized sentences and personally monitoring offenders takes time, and judges' court calendars are crowded. James Q. Wilson of the University of California at Los Angeles has suggested enlisting the police to help probation officers monitor offenders, particularly for the presence of weapons (Wilson, 1995). He recommends giving each police patrol officer a list of people on probation or parole who live on that officer's beat and then rewarding the police for making frequent stops to insure that the offenders are not carrying guns or violating other statutes. Police in Redmond, Washington have been involved in such an experiment since 1992, and while the program has not been formally evaluated, the police and corrections believe it has resulted in reduced crime (Morgan and Marris, 1994; Lehman, 2001).

The Problem of Incarceration as Punishment

But closer monitoring of probationers is only half the problem. The more difficult problem is finding jail and prison capacity to punish violators once they are discovered. Closely monitoring drug testing, for example, leads to many positive drug tests (Petersilia and Turner, 1993). Most local jails do not have sufficient space to incarcerate all drug users, wanting to prioritize space for violent offenders. The result is that probationers quickly learn that testing dirty for drugs, or violating other court-ordered conditions, has little consequence.

Oregon is trying to rectify this problem by allowing for a swift and certain, but short (two-to-three day) jail sentence on *every* probationer who tests positive for drugs (Parent et al., 1994; Benefiel, phone conversation with ACA staff, October 31, 2000). The notion is that offenders will find the term disruptive to their normal life and be deterred from further drug use. Sanctions may be gradually increased (up to one year of incarceration) with each subsequent failed drug test according to the discretion of the probation officer supervising the violating offender. An evaluation of the program by the National Council on Crime and Delinquency (Baird, Wagner, and DeComo, 1995) shows encouraging results in terms of increasing offender participation in treatment and lowering recidivism while under supervision.

The Delaware Department of Corrections noted that 60 percent of its violations from probation and parole were for technical reasons, putting significant strain on the state's jail and prison operation. Their solution was to build into the system an intermediate step between probation and incarceration by building Violation of Probation centers. In 2000, two such centers were operational, with a third in the planning stages. An offender usually ends up in the Violation of Probation center after being arrested by probation officers using an administrative warrant for technical violations of the conditions of supervision. Usually within one working day, the offender is placed on a special Violation of Probation court calendar reserved for the program. The intent is to transfer the offender as quickly as possible to the Violation of Probation center.

First-time offenders serve up to seven days; second-time offenders serve up to fourteen days; and repeat offenders can serve up to thirty days. There is no limit to the number of times an offender can be sent to the Violation of Probation center. The Violation of Probation philosophy is similar to that of boot camps. The days are highly regimented; the rules are strict; and the discipline is enforced without exception. The Delaware Commissioner of Correction wrote: "The goal of the Violation of Probation center is to fulfill the need for an immediate, harsh sanction for probation violators" (Taylor, 2000:185).

While empirical evidence as to the effects of these programs is scant, system officials believe that the programs serve to increase the certainty of punishment, while reserving scarce prison space for the truly violent. Importantly, experts believe that states with "intermediate" (nonprison) options for responding to less serious probation/parole violations are able to reduce new commitments to prison.

The Empirical Data on Probation

Unfortunately, debating the merits of these or other strategies is severely limited because we know so little about current probation practice. Assembling what is known about U.S. probation practices, so that public policy can be better informed, is the main purpose of this book.

Together, the data show that probation is seriously underfunded relative to prisons—a policy that is not only short-sighted but dangerous. Probationers in urban areas often receive little or no supervision, and the resulting recidivism rates are high for felons. But due to prison crowding, there is renewed interest in community-based sanctions, and recent evaluative evidence suggests that probation programs—properly designed and implemented—can be effective on a number of dimensions, including reducing recidivism.

There are several steps to achieving greater crime control over probationers. First, we must provide adequate financial resources to deliver programs that have been shown to work. Successful probation programs combine *both* treatment and surveillance, and are targeted toward appropriate offender subgroups. Current evidence suggests low-level drug offenders are prime candidates for enhanced probation programs. We then must work to garner more public support by convincing citizens that probation sanctions are punitive, and convincing the judiciary that offenders will be held accountable for their behavior. Over time, probation will demonstrate its effectiveness, both in terms of reducing the human toll that imprisonment exacts on those incarcerated, and reserving scarce resources to ensure that truly violent offenders remain in prison.

Organization of "Probation and Intermediate Sanctions in the United States"

Chapter 2 begins by describing U.S. juvenile and adult probation data sources, explaining briefly why the topic has received relatively little attention. Chapter 3 presents a brief history of probation in the United States, highlighting important milestones.

Chapter 4 summarizes probation in modern sentencing practice, discussing how the probation decision is made, the preparation of the presentence investigation, and the setting and enforcing of probation conditions. This section also describes the organization and funding of U.S. probation departments.

Chapter 5 describes current probation population characteristics. It reviews the growth in probation populations, and depicts what is known about offenders' crimes, court-ordered conditions, and supervision requirements. It also presents data detailing how the granting of probation varies across jurisdictions.

Chapter 6 is devoted to assessing probation outcomes by reviewing recidivism and alternative outcomes measures. Chapter 7 outlines several steps to reviving probation and achieving greater crime control over probationers.

CHAPTER TWO

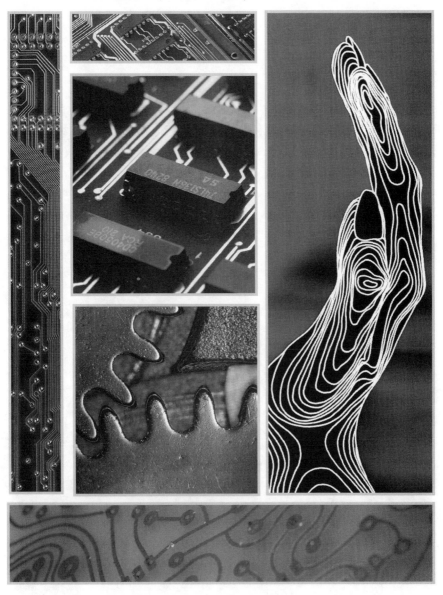

Sources of Probation Information

Probation receives little public scrutiny, not by intent but because the probation system is so complex and the data is scattered among hundreds of loosely connected agencies, each operating with a wide variety of rules and structures. Whereas one agency may be required to serve juvenile, misdemeanant, and felony offenders, another agency may handle only one type of offender. In some locations, probation officers run detention facilities and day-reporting centers, and in still others, they supervise pretrial offenders or even parolees, and run school-based prevention programs. The term "probation" has various meanings within multiple areas of corrections, and the volume and type of offenders on probation are quite large and varied.

Federal Data Collection

Virtually all probation information is national in scope and collected by agencies within the Office of Justice Programs, U.S. Department of Justice. There are only a few states (for example, Minnesota, Vermont, and North Carolina) that collect more detailed data on probationers, and very few probation agencies maintain their own research units. As a result, most states cannot describe the demographic or crime characteristics of probationers under their supervision. For example, California—which supervises nearly 300,000 adult probationers—is unable to provide the gender, age, or crime convictions of its probationers on the annual survey administered by the Bureau of Justice Statistics (Maquire and Pastore, 1995).

Data on Juvenile Probationers

Information on the number of youths placed on probation comes from the *Juvenile Court Statistics* series. This annual series collects information from all U.S.

courts with juvenile jurisdiction. Sponsored by the Office of Juvenile Justice and Delinquency Prevention (OJJDP) and analyzed by the National Center for Juvenile Justice (NCJJ), it describes the numbers of youths granted probation, and their underlying crime and demographic characteristics (*see* Puzzanchera et al., 2000).

In 1992, the Office of Juvenile Justice and Delinquency Prevention sponsored a nationwide survey of juvenile probation departments, collecting information on departments' sizes, organizations, and caseload sizes. Results of this survey are contained in Hurst and Torbet (1993).

Data on Adult Probationers

Nearly all existing national data describing adult probationers comes from two statistical series sponsored by the Bureau of Justice Statistics, the statistical arm of the U.S. Department of Justice. The first series, "Correctional Populations in the United States" (Bureau of Justice Statistics, 2000) collects annual counts and movements from all federal, state, and local adult probation agencies in the United States. Probationer information includes race, sex, and ethnicity, and provides the numbers on probation for felonies, misdemeanors, and driving while intoxicated. Data on the type of discharge is also obtained (in other words, successful completion or incarceration). This information has been collected by the Department of Justice since the mid-1970s.

The second series is the "National Judicial Reporting Program," a biennial sample survey, which compiles information on the sentences that felons receive in state courts nationwide and on the characteristics of felons. The latest information is reported in *State Court Sentencing of Convicted Felons, 1996* (Levin, Langan, and Brown, 2000) and is based on samples of all 3,195 counties nationwide. The information collected on convicted felons includes their age, race, gender, prior criminal record, length of sentence, and conviction offense.

Data on the organization of adult probation departments has been collected sporadically over the years by the National Institute of Justice (Comptroller General, 1976; Allen, Carlson, Parks, 1979; Nelson, Ohmart, and Harlow, 1978);

National Association of Criminal Justice Planners (Cunniff and Bergsmann, 1990; Cunniff and Shilton, 1991), the National Institute of Corrections (1993; 2000), and the Criminal Justice Institute (Camp and Camp, 1997, 1999, 2000). The Criminal Justice Institute, a private, nonprofit organization, has published, since 1990, selected probation data in *The Corrections Yearbook*.

The National Institute of Justice, the research arm of the U.S. Department of Justice, has sponsored nearly all of the basic and evaluation research conducted to date on adult probation. In recent years, these efforts have focused primarily on evaluating the effects of intermediate sanctions, programs that are more severe than routine probation but do not involve incarceration (for a review, *see* Tonry and Lynch, 1996).

Further Data Collection Needed

Beyond these minimal data, there is little systematic information on probation. We know almost nothing, for example, about the more than one million adult misdemeanants who are placed on probation—what were their crimes, what services did probation provide, and how many were rearrested? And except for the studies mentioned above, we do not have that type of information for adult felons or juveniles either. There are serious gaps in our knowledge, and what does exist is not easily accessible or summarized.

CHAPTER THREE

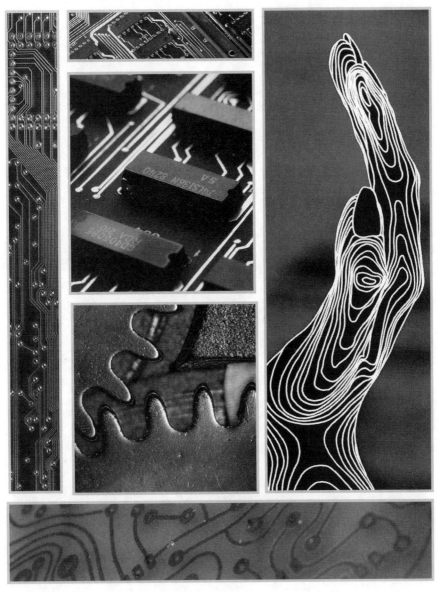

Origins and Evolution of Probation

Probation in the United States began in 1841 with the innovative work of John Augustus, a Boston bootmaker who was the first to post bail for a man charged with being a common drunk under the authority of the Boston Police Court. Mr. Augustus, a religious man of financial means, had some experience working with alcoholics. When the man appeared before the judge for sentencing, Mr. Augustus asked the judge to defer sentencing for three weeks and release the man into his custody. At the end of this brief probationary period, the offender convinced the judge of his reform and therefore received a nominal fine. The concept of probation had been born (Dressler, 1962).

From the beginning, the "helping" role of Augustus met with the scorn of law enforcement officials who wanted the offenders punished, not helped. But Augustus persisted, and the court gradually accepted the notion that not all offenders needed to be incarcerated. During the next fifteen years (from 1841 until his death in 1859), Augustus bailed out more than 1,800 persons in the Boston courts, making himself liable to the extent of $243,234 and preventing these individuals from being held in jail to await trial. Augustus is reported to have selected his candidates carefully, offering assistance "mainly to those who were indicted for their first offense, and whose hearts were not wholly depraved, but gave promise of better things" (Augustus, 1939). He provided his charges with aid in obtaining employment, an education, or a place to live, and also made an impartial report to the court.

Augustus reported great success with his charges, nearly all of whom were accused or convicted of violating Boston's vice or temperance laws. Of the first 1,100 offenders he discussed in his autobiography, he claimed only one had forfeited bond, and asserted that, with help, most of them eventually led upright lives (Augustus, 1939).

Early Probation Services

Buoyed by Augustus' example, Massachusetts quickly moved into the forefront of probation development. An experiment in providing services for children (resembling probation) was inaugurated in 1869. In 1878, Massachusetts was the first state to adopt a formal probation law for juveniles. Interestingly, it was also the concern for mitigating the harshness of penalties for children that led to the international development of probation (Hamai et al., 1995).

Public support for adult probation was much more difficult to achieve. It was not until 1901 that New York passed the first statute authorizing probation for adult offenders; more than twenty years later, Massachusetts passed its law for juvenile probationers (Latessa and Allen, 1997). By 1956, all states had adopted adult and juvenile probation laws.

John Augustus' early work provided the model for probation as we know it today. He originally conceived virtually every basic practice of probation. He was the first person to use the term "probation"—which derives from the Latin term *probatio*, meaning a "period of proving or trial." He developed the ideas of the presentence investigation, supervision conditions, social casework, reports to the court, and revocation of probation. Unfortunately, the visionary Augustus died destitute (Dressler, 1962).

Early Probation Officers

Initially, probation officers were volunteers who, according to Augustus, just needed to have a good heart. Early probation volunteer officers were often drawn from Catholic, Protestant, and Jewish congregations. In addition, police were reassigned to function as probation officers while continuing to draw their pay as municipal employees. But as the concept spread and the number of persons arrested increased, the need for presentence investigations and other court investigations increased, and the position of the volunteer probation officer was converted into a paid one (Dressler, 1962). The new officers hired were drawn largely from the law enforcement community—retired sheriffs and policemen—and they worked directly for the judge.

Gradually, the role of court support and probation officer became synonymous, and probation officers became "the eyes and ears of the local court." As Rothman observes, some years later, "probation developed in the United States very haphazardly, and with no real thought" (Rothman,1980: 244). Missions were unclear and often contradictory, and from the start there was tension between the law enforcement and rehabilitation purposes of probation (McAnany, Thomson, and Fogel, 1984). But most importantly, tasks were continually added to probation's responsibilities, while funding remained constant or declined. A 1979 survey (Fitzharris) found that probation departments were responsible for more than fifty different activities, including court-related civil functions (for example, stepparent adoption investigations and minority-age marriage investigations).

The Evolution of Probation Services

Between the 1950s and 1970s, U.S. probation evolved in relative obscurity. But a number of reports issued in the 1970s brought national attention to the inadequacy of probation services and their organization. The National Advisory Commission on Criminal Justice Standards and Goals (1973:112) stated that probation was the "brightest hope for corrections," but was "failing to provide services and supervision." In 1974, a widely publicized review of rehabilitation programs purportedly showed probation's ineffectiveness (Martinson,1974), and two years later, the U.S. Comptroller General's Office released a report concluding that probation as then practiced was a failure, and that the U.S. probation systems were "in crisis" (1976:3). They urged that "[s]ince most offenders are sentenced to probation, probation systems must receive adequate resources. But something more fundamental is needed. The priority given to probation in the criminal justice system must be reevaluated" (Comptroller General of the United States, 1976:74).

In recent years, probation agencies have struggled—with continued meager resources—to upgrade services and supervision. Important developments have included the widespread adoption of case classification systems and various types of intermediate sanctions (for example, electronic monitoring and intensive supervision). These programs have had varied success in reducing recidivism, but the evaluations have been instructive in terms of future program design. Significant events in the development of U.S. probation are contained in Table 1.

NIFICANT EVENTS IN THE DEVELOPMENT OF U.S. PROBATION

Year	Event
1841	— John Augustus introduces probation in the United States in Boston.
1878	— Massachusetts is the first state to adopt probation for juveniles.
1878-1938	— Thirty-seven states, the District of Columbia, and the federal government pass juvenile and adult probation laws.
1927	— All states but Wyoming have juvenile probation laws.
1954	— All states have juvenile probation laws.
1956	— All states have adult probation laws (Mississippi becomes the last state to pass authorizing legislation).
1973	— The National Advisory Commission on Criminal Justice Standards and Goals endorses more extensive use of probation. — Minnesota is the first state to adopt Community Corrections Act; eighteen states follow by 1995.
1974	— Martinson's widely publicized research purportedly proves that probation does not work.
1975	— U.S. Department of Justice conducts the first census of U.S. probationers. — Wisconsin implements first probation case classification system; American Probation and Parole Association founded.
1976	— U.S. Comptroller General's study of U.S. probation claims to reduce recidivism and costs.
1982	— Georgia's intensive supervision probation program claims to reduce recidivism and costs.
1983	— Electronic monitoring of offenders begins in New Mexico, followed by larger program in Florida.
1985	— RAND releases study of felony probationers showing high failure rates; replications follow, showing that probation services and effectiveness vary widely across nation.
1989	— General Accounting Office survey shows all fifty states have adopted intensive probation and other intermediate sanction programs.
1991	— U.S. Department of Justice funds nationwide intensive supervision demonstration and evaluation.
1993	— Program evaluations show probation without adequate surveillance and treatment is ineffective, but well-managed and adequately funded programs reduce recidivism.
1999	— "Broken Windows" model of probation, emphasizing that supervision is not effective when conducted solely in officers' offices, is endorsed by the American Probation and Parole Association.

Source: Compiled by the author.

CHAPTER FOUR

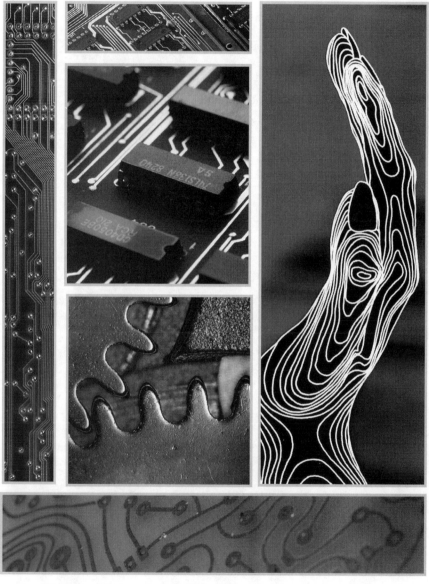

Probation and Modern Sentencing
Practices

Many of those arrested, and anyone who is convicted, come into contact with the probation department, whose officials operate with a great deal of discretionary authority and dramatically affect most subsequent justice processing decisions. Their input affects not only the subsequent liberties offenders will enjoy, but their decisions influence public safety. They recommend (within certain legal restraints) which offenders will be released back to their communities, and judges usually accept their sentence recommendations.

Probation's Influence throughout the Justice System

As shown in Figure 1 (*see* the following page), probation officials are involved in decision making long before sentencing, often beginning when the crime comes to the attention of the police. They usually perform the personal investigation to determine whether defendants will be released on their own recognizance or bail. Probation reports are the primary source of information the court uses to determine which cases will be deferred from formal prosecution. If deferred, probation officers also will supervise the diverted offender and their recommendation will be primary in deciding whether the offender successfully has complied with the diversionary sentence, and if so, no formal prosecution will occur.

For persons who violate court-ordered conditions, probation officers are responsible for deciding which violations will be brought to the attention of the courts, and what subsequent sanctions they should recommend. When the court grants probation, probation staff have great discretion about which court-ordered conditions to enforce and monitor. And when an offender goes to prison, the offender's initial security classification (and eligibility for parole) will be based on information contained in the presentence investigation. Finally, when offenders are released from jail or prison, probation staff often provide their community supervision.

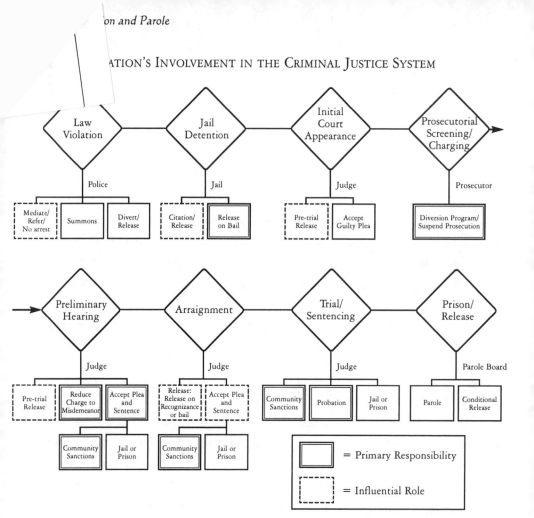

In fact, it is safe to say that no other justice agency is involved with the offenders and their cases as comprehensively as the probation department. Every other agency completes its work and hands the case over to the next decision maker. For example, the police arrest offenders, then hand them over to the prosecutor, who files charges and hands them to the judge, who sentences them and finally hands them to the warden who confines them. The probation department, however, interacts with all of these agencies, provides the data that influences each of their processing decisions, and takes charge of the offender's supervision at any point when the system decides to return the offender to the community (Of course, for parolees, parole officers usually assume this function). Figure 1 highlights the involvement of probation agencies throughout the justice system, showing its integral role in custody and supervision.

The Presentence Investigation Report

When most think of probation, they think of its *supervisory* function. But providing law enforcement agencies and the courts with the necessary information to make key processing decisions is the other major function of probation, commonly referred to as probation's *investigative* function.

From the point of arrest, information about the offenders' crime and criminal background is accumulated and eventually presented to the court if the case proceeds through prosecution and sentencing. This formal document is known as the presentence investigation (PSI) or presentence report (PSR).

The presentence investigation is the critically important document, since more than 90 percent of all felony convictions in the United States eventually are resolved through a guilty plea (Bureau of Justice Statistics, 2000a), and the major decision of the court is whether imprisonment will be imposed. A survey by the National Institute of Corrections found that half of all states require a presentence investigation in all felony cases; the presentence investigation is discretionary for felonies in another sixteen states. Only two states require a presentence investigation prior to disposition in misdemeanor cases (National Institute of Corrections, 1993). Nationally, probation officers wrote presentence investigations for 64 percent of all felons, which represented almost half of all probationers in 1995 (Bonczar, 1997). Where presentence investigations are discretionary, the option of requesting them usually rests with the courts.

Research repeatedly has shown that judge's knowledge of the defendant usually is limited to the information contained in the presentence investigation and, as a result, there is a high correlation between the recommendation of the probation officer and the judge's sentence. Research by the American Justice Institute (1981), using samples from representative probation departments throughout the United States, found that recommendations for probation were adopted by the sentencing judge between 66 and 95 percent of the time. In 1999, the U. S. Department of Justice reported that 80 percent of 1995 probationers with presentence investigations had received recommendations for probation (Bonczar, 1997).

The probation department's presentence investigation typically includes information on the seriousness of the crime, the defendant's risk, the defendant's circumstance, a summary of the legally permissible sentencing options, and a recommendation for or against prison. If recommending prison, the presentence investigation recommends sentence length; and if recommending probation, the presentence investigation recommends sentence length and the conditions to be imposed.

Some have asserted that the introduction of sentencing guidelines—which require calculations based on details of the crime and prior criminal record—have increased the importance of the presentence investigation and the role and responsibility of the probation officer, particularly at the federal level. Others have argued just the contrary: "the percentage of cases in which probation orders are issued after consideration of . . . (presentence investigations) has been declining in recent years, in part because of the rising use of sentencing guidelines." (Office of Justice Programs, 1998: xiii). Whatever one decides are the merits and shortcomings of sentencing by guidelines—where individualized conditions give way to standard conditions—most agree on the value of probation's input, especially regarding offender agency accountability.

While the presentence investigation is initially prepared to aid the sentencing judge, once prepared it becomes a critically important document to justice officials throughout the system, and is the basis of most criminological research studies. As Abadinsky (1997:105) noted, its most common uses are as follows:

- Serving as the basis for the initial risk/needs classification probation officers use to assign an offender to a supervision caseload and treatment plan

- Assisting jail and prison personnel in their classification and treatment programs

- Furnishing parole authorities with information pertinent to consideration for parole and release planning

- Providing a source of information for research studies

Factors Influencing Who Is Sentenced to Probation Versus Prison

The most important purpose of the presentence investigation is to assist in making the prison/probation decision. Generally speaking, the more serious the offenses, the greater the likelihood of a prison term. For example, in 1996, only 21 percent of all violent offenses (such as murders and assaults) led to probation sentences. On the other hand, the remaining 79 percent led to incarceration in jail or prison. Probation was a more likely sentence for felonies such as property offenses (38 percent), weapons offenses (33 percent), and other nonviolent offenses like vandalism (37 percent) (Levin, Langan, and Brown, 2000). For 1999 federal cases, the trend is even more striking: only about 200 of the approximately 2,700 violent offense convictions led to probation or mixed sentences (Bureau of Justice Statistics, 2001). But exactly what crime and/or offender characteristics are used by the court to assess "seriousness?"

Petersilia and Turner (1986) analyzed the criminal records and case files of approximately 16,500 males, each of whom had been convicted of selected felony crimes in one of seventeen California counties in 1980. The researchers coded detailed information about the offender's crimes, criminal backgrounds, and how their case was processed (for example, private or public attorney). The purpose was to identify the specific factors that distinguished who was granted probation (with or without a jail term) and who was sentenced to prison, when both persons had been convicted of the same penal code, in the same county, and in the same year. They found that a person was more likely to receive a prison sentence if the individual:

- had two or more conviction counts (in other words, was convicted of multiple charges)

- had two or more prior criminal convictions

- was on probation or parole at the time of the arrest

- was a drug addict

- used a weapon during the commission of the offense or seriously injured the victims

For all offenses except assault, offenders having three or more of these characteristics had an 80 percent or greater probability of going to prison in California, regardless of the type of crime for which they currently were convicted (Petersilia and Turner, 1986).

After controlling for these "basic factors," the researchers also found that having a private (versus public) attorney could reduce a defendant's chances of imprisonment (this was true except for drug cases, where the type of attorney made no difference). Obtaining pretrial release also lessened the probability of going to prison, whereas going to trial increased that probability (Petersilia and Turner, 1986).

But while such factors predicted about 75 percent of the sentencing decisions in the study, they did not explain the remainder. Thus, Petersilia and Turner (1986) concluded that in about 25 percent of the cases studied, those persons sent to prison could not be effectively distinguished in terms of their crimes or criminal backgrounds from those receiving probation. These data suggest that many offenders who are granted felony probation are indistinguishable in terms of their crimes or criminal record from those who are imprisoned (or vice versa).

Setting and Enforcing the Conditions of Probation

For those offenders granted probation, the court decides which specific conditions will be included in the probation contract between the offender and the court. In actual practice, when a judge sentences an offender to probation, he or she often combines the probation term with a suspended sentence, whereby the judge sentences a defendant to prison or jail and then suspends the sentence in favor of probation. In this way, the jail or prison term has been legally imposed, but simply held in abeyance to be reinstated if the offender fails to abide by the probation conditions (Latessa and Allen, 1997). Offenders are presumed to be more motivated to comply with the conditions of probation by knowing what awaits them should they fail to comply.

In addition to deciding whether to impose a sentence of incarceration and then "suspend" it in favor or probation (or to sentence to probation directly), the judge makes a number of other highly important, but discretionary decisions. The judge must decide whether to impose a jail or prison term along with probation. This is commonly referred to as "split sentencing," and nationally, probation is combined with a jail or prison term in 27 percent of felony cases (Levin, Langan, and Brown, 2000). Some states use split sentencing more frequently. For example, 60 percent of persons sentenced to probation in Minnesota are required to serve some jail time (Minnesota Sentencing Guidelines Commission, 1996), as are nearly 80 percent of felons in California (California Department of Justice, 1995). Nationally, just over half of the probationers received split sentences in 1998 (Bonczar and Glaze, 1999). The average jail sentence for male felony probationers is six months, while the average length of felony probation is forty months (Levin, Langan, and Brown, 2000).

It is the judge's responsibility to enumerate the conditions the probationer must abide by in order to remain in the community. The particular conditions of an offender's probation contract usually are recommended by probation officers and contained in the presentence investigation. But they also may be designed by the judge, and judges are generally free to construct any terms of probation they deem necessary. Judges also often authorize the setting of "such other conditions as the probation officer may deem proper to impose" or may leave the mode of implementation a condition (such as a method of treatment) to the discretion of the probation officer.

The judge's (and probation officer's) required conditions usually fall into one of three realms.

- *Standard conditions,* imposed on all probationers, include such requirements as reporting to the probation office, notifying the agency of any change of address, remaining gainfully employed, and not leaving the jurisdiction without permission.

- *Punitive conditions* are usually established to reflect the seriousness of the offense, and increase the painfulness of probation. Examples are fines, community service, victim restitution, house arrest, and drug testing (American Correctional Association, 2001).

- *Treatment conditions* are imposed to force probationers to deal with significant problems or needs, such as substance abuse treatment, family counseling, or vocational training.

The Supreme Court has held that probation should not be considered a form of "prison without walls," but rather a period of conditional liberty that is protected by due process (McShane and Krause, 1993: 93). In that vein, the courts have ruled that each probation condition must not infringe on the basic rights of the person being supervised. Case law has established that there are four general elements in establishing the legal validity of a probation condition. Each imposed probation condition must:

- serve a *legitimate purpose*—either to protect society or lead to the rehabilitation of the offender.

- be *clear*—with language that is explicit, outlining specifically what can or cannot be done so that the average person can know exactly what is expected.

- be *reasonable*—not excessive in its expectations.

- be *constitutional*—while probationers do have a diminished expectation of certain privileges, they retain basic human freedoms such as religion, speech, and marriage.

In legal terms, the probation conditions form a contract between the offender and the court. An excellent discussion of the legal basis for probation and enforcing probation conditions can be found in Klein (1997). The contract states the conditions, at least theoretically, that the offender must abide by to remain in the community. The court requires that the probation officer provide the defendant with a written statement setting forth all the conditions to which the sentence is subject. The offender signs the contract, and the probation officer is the "enforcer" of the contract, responsible for notifying the court when the contract is not being fulfilled.

Violating the Conditions of Probation

Should a defendant violate a probation condition at any time prior to the expiration of the term of probation, the court after a hearing pursuant to certain rules (which include written notification of charges) may:

- retain him or her on probation, with or without extending the term or modifying or enlarging the conditions.

- revoke the sentence of probation and impose any other sentence that was available at the time of the initial sentencing (for example, prison or jail).

As mentioned previously, a suspended sentence often is issued along with probation, and upon revocation, judges may order the original sentence to be imposed. When a suspended sentence is reinstated, judges may decide to give credit for probation time already served, or they may require the complete original incarceration term to be served.

Over the years, the number of offenders who have special conditions attached to probation has increased (Clear, 1994). The public's more punitive mood, combined with inexpensive drug testing and a higher number of probationers having substance abuse problems, undoubtedly contributes to the increase in the number of conditions imposed on probationers. More stringent conditions increase the chances of failure (Petersilia and Turner, 1993). According to the Bureau of Justice Statistics, a lower percentage of offenders are successfully completing their probation terms. In 1986, 74 percent of those who exited probation successfully completed their terms; in 1992, the figure was 67 percent, and by 1998, that figure had dropped to 59 percent (Langan, 1996; Bonczar and Glaze, 1999).

Bonczar's 1997 statistical report on probationers showed that more than 60 percent of 1995 probationers participated in some special supervision or program (shown in Figure 2), the most common being drug testing.

FIGURE 2: SPECIAL CONDITIONS IMPOSED ON ADULT FELONY PROBATIONERS

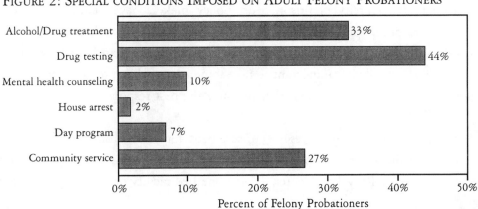

Other analysis by Langan (1994) showed that many probationers failed to satisfy their probation-ordered conditions. He found that half of all probationers simply did not comply with the court-ordered terms of their probation, and only 50 percent of the known violators ever went to jail or prison for their noncompliance. Langan concluded (1994:791) ". . . sanctions are not vigorously enforced."

Taxman and Byrne (1994) reanalyzing a national sample of felons placed on probation and tracked by the Bureau of Justice Statistics for two years (Dawson, 1990) discovered that even probation absconders (in other words, those who fail to report) are often not punished. They found that, on any one day, about 10 to 20 percent of adult felony probationers were on abscond status, their whereabouts unknown. While warrants usually were issued for their arrest, no agency actively invests time in finding the offenders and serving the warrants. They concluded that, practically speaking, as long as offenders are not rearrested, they are not violators.

Even though many court-ordered conditions are not actively enforced, the probation population is so large, that even revoking a small percentage of them or revoking all those who are rearrested, can have a dramatic impact on prison admissions. In fact, 1999 estimates show that more than 40 percent of all new prison admissions are probation and parole failures (Camp and Camp, 1999). Michigan, for example, reported that in 1999, more than one half of all prison admissions were either probation or parole violators. In Arizona, the figure was more than 60 percent (Camp and Camp, 2000).

Due to the scarcity of prison beds, policy makers have begun to wonder whether revoking probationers and parolees for technical violations (in other words, infractions of the conditions of supervision, rather than for a new crime) makes sense. While it is important to take some action when probation violations are discovered, it is not obvious that prison is the best response.

Several states, trying to reserve prison beds for violent offenders, are now structuring the courts' response to technical violations. Missouri has opened up the Kansas City Recycling Center, a forty-one-bed facility operated by a private contractor to deal exclusively with technical violators who have been recommended for revocation (Herman, 1993). Mississippi and Georgia use boot camp programs for probation violators (Grubbs 1993; Prevost, Rhine, and Jackson, 1993; www.dcor.state.ga.us/pdf/fy00; www.mdoc.state.ms.us/services/red.htm). While empirical evidence is scant as to the effects of these programs, system officials believe that the programs serve to increase the certainty of punishment, while reserving scarce prison space for the truly violent (Rhine, 1993).

Probation Caseloads and Contact Levels

The most common measure of probation's workload is caseload size, or the number of offenders assigned to each probation officer. Published reports normally divide the number of probation department employees or line officers by the number of adult probationers under supervision to indicate average caseload size. Over the years, probation caseloads have grown from what was thought to be an ideal size of 30:1 in the mid-1970s (President's Commission on Law Enforcement, 1972) to today, where the average adult regular supervision caseload is reported to be 139:1 (Camp and Camp, 2000). In Rhode Island, where 1 in 33 adult residents is on probation, there is an average caseload of 363:1, which is one of the highest in the nation (Associated Press, 2001).

The "average caseload size" figure is misleading and vastly overstates the number of officers available for offender supervision. First, as Cunniff and Bergsmann's study (1990) showed, not all probation employees or even line officers are assigned to offender supervision. On average, Cunniff and Bergsmann (1990) found that in a typical U.S. probation department:

- Only 52 percent of a typical probation department's staff are line officers, 48 percent are clerical, support staff, and management (such high clerical staffing is required because a third to a half of all clerical personnel type presentence investigations for the court).

- Of line probation officers, only about 17 percent of them supervise adult felons. The remaining officers supervise juveniles (half of all U.S. adult probation departments also have responsibility for supervising juveniles), and 11 percent prepare presentence investigations.

There were more than 60,000 probation employees in 1999 (Camp and Camp, 1999). If 23 percent of them (or 11,500 officers) were supervising 3.7 million adult probationers, then the average U.S. adult probation caseload in 1999 would equal 321 offenders for each line officer.

A survey (Thomas, 1993) of juvenile probation officers responsible for supervision showed that U.S. juvenile caseloads range between 2 and 200 cases, with a typical (median) active caseload of 41. The optimal caseload suggested by juvenile probation officers was thirty cases.

Of course, offenders are not supervised on "average" caseloads. Rather, probation staff use a variety of risk and needs classification instruments to identify those offenders needing more intensive supervision and/or services. Developing these "risk/need" classification devices occupied probation personnel throughout the 1970s, and their use is now routine throughout the United States (for a review, *see* Clear, 1988). Unfortunately, while risk assessments are better able to identify offenders more likely to reoffend, funds are usually insufficient to implement the level of supervision predicted by the classification instrument (Jones, 1996).

Recent surveys show 85.5 percent of *all* U.S. adult probationers are supervised on regular caseloads, whereas 2.7 percent are on intensive supervision and 8.8 percent are on specialized caseloads, such as electronic monitoring or boot camps (Camp and Camp, 2000). Again, however, these numbers do not tell us much about the actual contact levels received by felons. The best data on this subject comes from the Langan and Cunniff (1992) study tracking felony probationers. They report that about 10 percent of *felony* probationers are placed on intensive caseloads, where administrative guidelines suggest probation officers should have contact with probationers nine times per month (Table 2). The authors note that this initial classification level does not necessarily mean that they got that level of service, but, rather, they were assigned to a caseload having that administrative standard.

The Langan and Cunniff (1992) study also provides information on supervision level, relative to conviction crime, and county of conviction. They report

TABLE 2: FELONY PROBATIONERS' INITIAL SUPERVISION LEVELS

Supervision Level	Prescribed Number of Contacts	Percent of Caseload
Intensive	9 per month	10
Maximum	3 per month	32
Medium	1 per month	37
Minimum	1 per 3 months	12
Administrative	None required	9

Source: Langan and Cunniff, 1992.

that, across all the sites and felony crimes studied, about 20 percent of adult felony probationers are assigned to caseloads requiring no personal contact.

In large urban counties, the situation is particularly acute, and some data may not reflect the seriousness of the situation. Take, for example, the Los Angeles County Probation Department, the largest probation department in the world. In fiscal year 2000, its 1,869 probation officers and agents were responsible for supervising 96,388 adult and juvenile offenders. Compared to fiscal year 1994, this data constitutes a 25 percent increase in officers and a 12.5 decrease in probationers (American Correctional Association, 2001). However, since the mid-1970s, county officials have continually cut their budgets, while the number of persons granted probation and the number of required presentence investigations has grown (Nidorf, 1996).

The result is that in 1998/1999, 65 percent of all Los Angeles probationers (under both field and special services) were supervised on an "Automated Minimum Supervision Caseload" (AMSC). In these caseloads, no services, supervision, or personal contact is provided. Instead, these persons are simply required to participate in a video orientation program, mail-in notification once or twice a month, and be subject to computers monitoring their compliance. Data published on the department's website calculates the automated minimum supervision caseload probationer-to-deputy probation officer ratio at 1,000 to 1 (Los Angeles County Probation Department, 2001). A more detailed study found that, on any given day, there are nearly 10,000 violent offenders (convicted of murder, rape, assault, kidnapping, and/or robbery) being supervised by probation officers in Los Angeles, and about half of them are on automated minimum case-loads with no reporting requirements (Los Angeles County Planning Committee, 1996). Even those classified as "High Risk Offenders," who receive more supervision and services, are supervised at a ratio of 200 probationers per 1 probation officer (Los Angeles County Probation Department, 2001).

The Organization of Probation

Probation is basically a state and local activity, with the federal government providing technical support, data gathering, and funding for innovative programs and their evaluation. Probation is administered by more than 2,000 separate agencies, and there is no uniform structure (Abadinsky, 1997). As the National Institute of Corrections observed, "Probation was established in nearly as many patterns as there are states, and they have since been modified by forces unique to each state and each locality" (1993: v). The result is that probation services in the United States differ in terms of whether they are delivered by the executive or the judicial branch of government, how services are funded, and whether probation services are primarily a state or a local function. While a detailed discussion of these issues is beyond the scope of this essay, interested readers are referred to the National Institute of Corrections (1999) report *State Organizational Structures for Delivering Adult Probation Services.*

Centralized or Decentralized Probation?

The centralization issue concerns the location of authority to administer probation services. Proponents of probation argue that judicially administered probation (usually on a county level) promotes diversity. Nelson, Ohmart, and Harlow (1978) suggest that an agency administered by a city or county instead of a state is smaller, more flexible, and better able to respond to the unique problems of the community. And because decentralized probation draws its support from its community and local government, it can offer more appropriate supervision for its clients and make better use of existing resources. It is also predicted that if the state took over probation, it might be assigned a lower level of priority than it would be if it remained a local, judicially controlled service.

Over time, adult probation services moved from the judicial to the executive branch, and now located exclusively in the judicial branch in [...] states (*see* Figure 3). However, more than half of the agencies [...] probation services are administered on the local level. (Fortur [...] tration of parole is much less complex: one agency per state [...] executive branch).

FIGURE 3: JURISDICTIONAL ARRANGEMENTS FOR ADULT PROBATION BY STATE

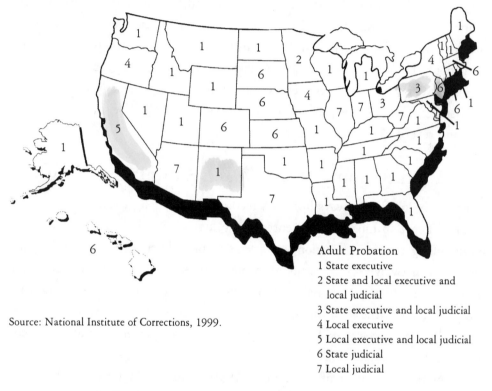

Source: National Institute of Corrections, 1999.

Adult Probation
1 State executive
2 State and local executive and local judicial
3 State executive and local judicial
4 Local executive
5 Local executive and local judicial
6 State judicial
7 Local judicial

The trend in adult probation is towards centralization, where authority for a state's probation activities is placed in a single statewide administrative body (National Institute of Corrections, 1993). More than half of the states administer probation through the states' department of corrections (National Institute of Corrections, 1999). In 1996, three-quarters of all states located adult probation in the executive branch, where services and funding were centralized. Proponents of this approach assert that all other human services and correctional subsystems are located within the executive branch; program budgeting can be better coordinated; and judges, trained in law, not administration, are not well equipped to administer probation services (Abadinsky 1997:35). Even in those county-based

.. systems, states usually have created an oversight agency for better
ınation and uniformity of probation services—California is currently the
ıly state operating probation locally without a state oversight agency (Parent et
al., 1994).

As Clear and Cole (1997) point out, there is no optimal probation organization. In jurisdictions with a tradition of strong and effective local probation programming, decentralized services make sense. In states that typically have
provided services through centralized, large scale bureaucracies, perhaps probation should be part of such services. One thing is for sure, as probation receives
greater attention—and its services and supervision are more closely scrutinized—
the issue of who oversees probation, and who is responsible for standards, training, and revocation policy will become central.

Probation Funding: State Versus County Funding

Probation funding always has been recognized as woefully inadequate, given
its prominence in modern U.S. sentencing practices. While states have become
more willing to fund probation, counties still provide the primary funding for
probation in twelve states, although some of these agencies receive significant
state support. In the National Institute of Corrections 1993 survey, California
counties received the least amount of state assistance, ranging from a low of 9
percent in Los Angeles and San Diego, to a high of 14 percent in San Francisco.
State funds are available only to counties which comply with state training standards (National Institute of Corrections, 1999). Counties in Texas, on the other
hand, received some of the largest shares of state assistance (Dallas received 50
percent of its operating budget from the state).

Some states have used other means to upgrade the quality of probation services and funding. Community Corrections Acts (CCAs) are mechanisms by which
state funds are granted to local governments to foster local sanctions to be used
in lieu of state prison. Today, almost half of the states have enacted Community
Corrections Acts and the evidence suggests that Community Corrections Acts
have encouraged some good local probation programs, but have been less successful at reducing commitments to state prison or improving coordination of

state and local programs (Shilton, 1995; Parent, 1995; Harris, 2001). Still, interest in the Community Corrections Act concept—and other state "subsidies" to upgrade probation through decentralization, deinstitutionalization, and increased citizen participation—is growing across the United States.

Arizona probation probably has the most ideal system. In 1987, the state legislature wrote into statute that felony probation caseloads could not exceed sixty offenders to one probation officer. And, they allocated state funding to maintain that level of service. As a result, probation departments in Arizona are nationally recognized to be among the best, providing their offenders with both strict surveillance and needed treatment services.

Annual Costs Per Probationer

The *Corrections Yearbook* reports that the 1999 daily costs spent for probationers on regular supervision in the United States ranged from $1.24 in Georgia to $3.50 in Illinois, with an average cost of $2.11 per day. For intensive supervision, the costs ranged from a daily high of $20.00 in New Jersey to a low of $2.50 in Rhode Island, with an average of $9.66 over the sixteen states reporting (Camp and Camp, 2000). But such numbers are rather meaningless, since we do not know what factors were considered in reaching that cost estimate. One system actually may compute the average cost per offender, per day on the basis of services rendered and officers' salaries, whereas other jurisdictions simply may divide the total operating budget by the number of clients served. Still others may figure into the equation the costs of various private contracts for treatment and drug testing. In short, there is no standard formula for computing probationer costs, but funds are known to be inadequate.

Since its beginnings, probation continually has been asked to take on greater numbers of probationers and conduct a greater number of presentence investigations, all the while experiencing stable or declining funding. As Clear and Braga write: "Apparently, community supervision has been seen as a kind of elastic resource that could handle whatever numbers of offenders the system required it to" (Clear and Braga, 1995:423).

From 1977 to 1990, prison, jail, parole, and probation populations all about tripled in size. Yet, only spending for prisons and jails had increased expenditures. In 1990, prison and jail spending accounted for two cents of every state and local dollar spent—twice the amount spent in 1977. Spending for probation and parole accounted for two-tenths of one cent of every dollar spent in 1990—unchanged from what it was in 1977 (Langan, 1994). Today, although two-thirds of all persons convicted are in the community, much smaller proportions of correctional budgets go to supervise them. Virginia's budget allocates more than a third, Iowa's budget designates almost a quarter, but many states (including Alabama, California, Illinois, Mississippi, and New Jersey) allocate around or less than one tenth of their correctional budget to community corrections (American Correctional Association, 2001).

Fines and Fees

As part of the conditions of probation, many jurisdictions are including various offender-imposed fees which, when collected, are used to support the probation department. These fees are levied for a variety of services including the preparation of presentence reports, electronic monitoring, work release programs, drug counseling, and regular probation supervision. By 1992, more than half of the states allowed probation departments to charge fees to probationers, ranging anywhere from $10 to $40 per month, usually with a sliding scale for those unable to pay (Finn and Parent, 1992). In 2000, West Virginia and Connecticut enacted laws allowing courts and agencies to charge probationers to help defray the cost of electronic monitoring. Also, in 2000, other states which passed legislation that address offender fees for probation or diversion programs included California, Colorado, Hawaii, Kentucky, Louisiana, New Mexico, Tennessee, and Washington (Lyons, 2001).

Finn and Parent (1992), in a National Institute of Justice study of fines, found that despite a common perception of the criminal as penniless and unemployable, most offenders on probation who have committed misdemeanors—and even many who have committed felonies—can afford reasonable monthly supervision fees. Texas, for example, has been highly successful in generating probation fees. Probationers there are required to pay a standard maximum monthly fee of $40 plus extra for the victims' fund (Camp and Camp, 1999). In 2000, Texas spent about $325 million to supervise probationers, and collected $100 million in fees (American Correctional Association, 2001).

Taxpayers applaud such efforts and they also may teach offenders personal responsibility, but the practice causes dilemmas concerning whether to revoke probation for nonpayment. The courts have ruled that probation cannot be revoked when indigent offenders have not paid their fees or restitution (*Bearden v. Georgia*, 1983).

CHAPTER FIVE

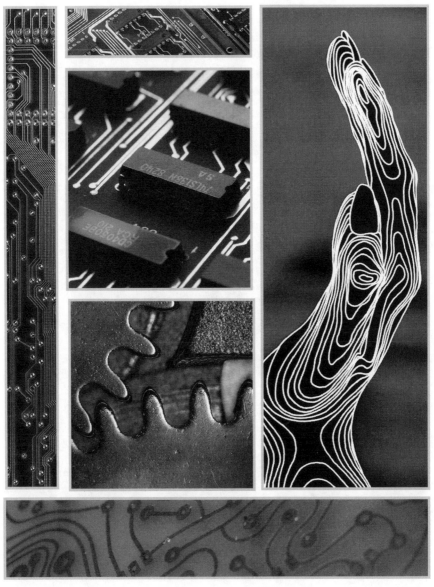

Characteristics and Risks of the Current
Probation Population

Probation was never intended to serve as a major criminal sanction. It was designed for first-time offenders who were not too deeply involved in crime, and for whom individualized treatment and casework could make a difference. But, as shown below, things have changed considerably.

Profile of Persons Placed on Probation: Size of the Probation Population

In 1996, the Bureau of Justice Statistics reported that U.S. judges sentence to probation or probation with jail 80 percent of all adults convicted of misdemeanors (crimes normally punishable by less than a year incarceration), and about 60 percent of all adults convicted of felonies (crimes punishable by more than one year in prison)—or fully two-thirds of all persons convicted of a crime (Bureau of Justice Statistics, 1996). They estimated that there were a record number of 3,773,600 adults on probation at year's end 1999, an increase of more than 8 percent over the previous year (*see* Figure 4, on the following page).

Figure 4 also shows a consistent three-to-one ratio between probationers and prisoners over the past decade. An interesting analysis by Zvekic (1996) shows that the United States and other Western European countries' preference for probation versus prison sentencing is not shared by some other countries, most notably Japan, Israel, and Scotland. For example, the ratio of imprisonment to probation in Japan is four-to-one.

The Bureau of Justice Statistics also reports that the southern states in the United States generally have the highest per capita ratio of probationers—reporting 2,170 probationers per 100,000 adults at year end 1999 (Bureau of Justice

FIGURE 4: ADULTS IN PRISON AND JAIL, AND ON PROBATION OR PAROLE, 1980-1999

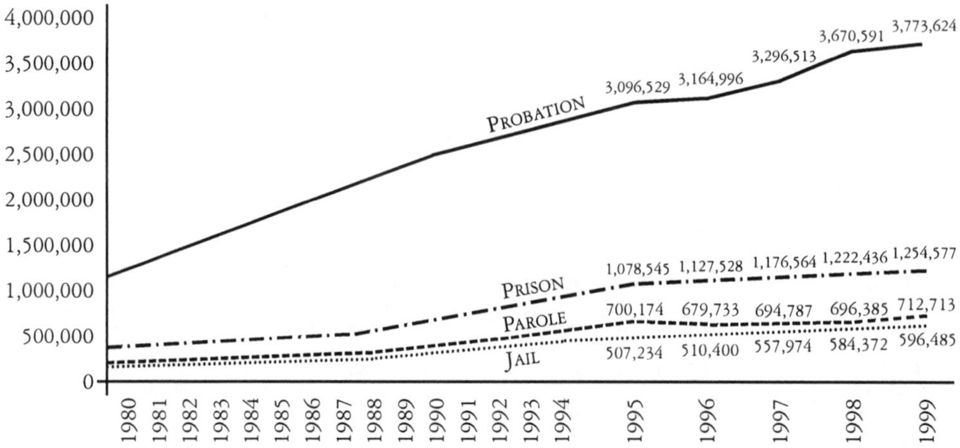

Source: Bureau of Justice Statistics (2000b).

Statistics, 2000b). In terms of sheer numbers of probationers, Texas has the largest adult probation population (about 447,100), followed by California (about 332,414). In Texas, 3.1 percent of all adults were on probation at the end of 1999 (Bureau of Justice Statistics, 2000b).

If probation were being used primarily as an alternative to incarceration, one might expect to find that the states that imposed more probationary sentences would have lower than average incarceration rates and vice versa. This is not the case. Generally, states with a relatively high per capita imprisonment rate also have a relatively high per capita use of probation. Texas, for example, had one of the highest state imprisonment rates in the nation (second only to Louisiana) and the highest rate of probation impositions in 1999 (Beck, 2000). Similarly, Southern states in 1999 generally placed persons on probation at the nation's highest rate, and they also incarcerated more than the rest of the nation (Bureau of Justice Statistics, 2000b; Beck, 2000).

Profile of Persons Placed on Probation: Demographic Characteristics and Conviction Crimes

More than 50 percent of all offenders on probation in 1998 had been convicted of a felony, and 40 percent were on probation for a misdemeanor. Nearly one in every six probationers had been convicted of driving while intoxicated—which could be either a felony or misdemeanor (Bonczar and Glaze, 1999).

Women made up 21 percent of the nation's probationers, a larger proportion than for any other correctional population. Approximately 64 percent of adults on probation were white, and 35 percent were black. Hispanics, who may be of any race, represented 15 percent of probationers (Bonczar and Glaze, 1999). These percentages have remained relatively constant since the Bureau of Justice Statistics began collecting the data in 1978 (Langan, 1996).

While the Bureau of Justice Statistics does not routinely collect the conviction crimes of probationers, they undertook a special *Census of Probation and Parole, 1991* (Bureau of Justice Statistics, 1992) where such information was obtained for a nationally representative sample of adult probationers (felons and misdemeanors combined). The conviction crimes of adult probationers are contained in Figure 5.

While we know less about the characteristics of juvenile probationers, Puzzanchera et al. (2000) reports that in 1997, 37 percent (645,600) of all formally and informally handled delinquency cases disposed of by juvenile courts resulted in probation. Probation was the most severe disposition in more than

FIGURE 5: ADULTS ON PROBATION BY CONVICTION CRIME TYPE

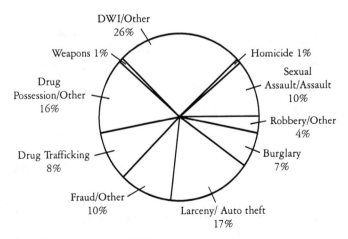

Source: Bureau of Justice Statistics, (1992).

half (55 percent) of adjudicated delinquency cases, with annual proportions remaining fairly constant for the ten-year period 1988-1997.

Figure 6 shows the growth in juvenile probation populations, and their under-lying offense. Remember that this growth in juvenile probation populations has occurred even though a number of serious juvenile cases are being waived to adult court for prosecution and sentencing (Puzzanchera et al., 2000). Judicial waivers increased 73 percent between 1988 and 1994, but decreased 28 percent between 1994 and 1997. Nonetheless, between 1988 and 1997, waivers increased by 25 percent. Waivers to adult court are still estimated to be less than 1 percent of all petitioned cases filed in juvenile court (Puzzanchera et al., 2000).

FIGURE 6: NUMBER OF JUVENILES IN THE UNITED STATES ON PROBATION BY YEAR AND CRIME

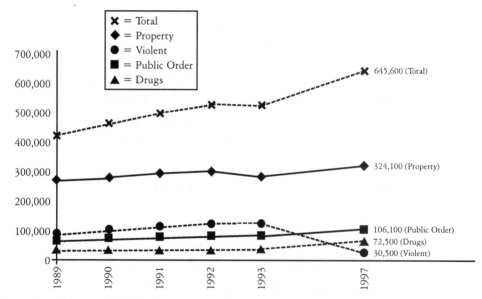

Source: Puzzanchera et al. (2000).

The Variability and Prevalence of Probation Sentencing

As noted earlier, the decision to grant probation is highly discretionary within certain legal boundaries, and practices vary considerably within and among states. Cunniff and Shilton (1991), in a study of more than 12,000 cases sentenced to probation in 1986 in 32 large jurisdictions, found that among the participating jurisdictions, the percent of all sentences involving probation ranged from a low of 30 percent in New York County (Manhattan) to a high of 75 percent in Hennepin County (Minneapolis).

Cunniff and Shilton (1991) suggest some of the variation is due to sentencing laws under which these jurisdictions function and their justice environment. They report that courts in determinate-sentencing states (with no parole board) tend to use probation more frequently than courts in indeterminate-sentencing states (with parole boards). Presumably, in indeterminate states, parole boards will release early the less serious and less dangerous offenders—thus reducing the length of prison time served for less serious offenders. But in determinate-sentencing states, prison terms are fixed and parole boards have little ability to reduce the length of stay courts impose. Apparently, judges are less willing to sentence to prison when the length of the term is fixed.

Studies also have shown that judges are more willing to place felons on probation when they perceive that the probation department can monitor the offender closely and that community resources are sufficient to address some of the offender's underlying problems (Frank, Cullen, and Cullen, 1987). Minnesota, Washington, and Arizona—the three states identified by Cunniff and Shilton (1991) as utilizing probation most frequently—are well known for delivering good probation supervision and having adequate resources to provide treatment and services.

Some of the variability in granting probation, however, also must be due to the underlying distribution of offense categories within these jurisdictions. For example, it may be that the robberies committed in one location are much less serious than those committed in another. However, reanalysis of a data set collected by RAND researchers, where offense seriousness was statistically controlled, still revealed a wide disparity among jurisdictions in their use of straight probation (in other words, without a jail term). Klein and his colleagues examined adjudication outcomes of defendants from fourteen large urban jurisdictions across the country in 1986, where all of the defendants were charged with stranger-to-stranger

FIGURE 7: PERCENT OF CONVICTED RESIDENTIAL BURGLARS AND ARMED ROBBERS GRANTED STRAIGHT PROBATION

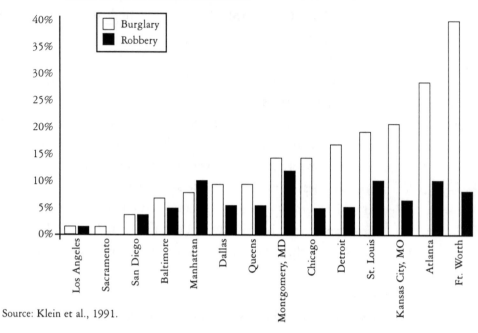

Source: Klein et al., 1991.

armed robberies and residential burglaries (Klein et al., 1991). They found that the granting of straight probation, even for felons convicted of similar crimes, varies substantially across the nation, particularly for burglary (*see* Figure 7). The figures for the California counties are particularly low because California commonly uses split sentences (probation plus jail) for felony crimes.

This demonstrated variability in the granting of probation is important. It suggests that the underlying probation population and the services they need and supervision risks they pose are vastly different, depending on the jurisdiction studied.

As noted above, states vary considerably in their use of probation. The main reason is that there are no national guidelines for granting probation, or limiting its use. Rather, generally speaking, the court is supposed to grant probation when the defendant does not pose a risk to society or need correctional supervision, and if the granting of probation would not underrate the seriousness of the crime (American Bar Association, 1970). Until recently, those broad guidelines were interpreted with great discretion.

TABLE 3: FELONY SENTENCES IMPOSED BY STATE AND FEDERAL COURTS BY OFFENSE, UNITED STATES, 1996

Most serious conviction offense	Total	Percent of felons sentenced to incarceration			
		Total	Prison	Jail	Probation
All offenses	100%	69%	38%	31%	31%
Violent offenses	100%	79%	57%	22%	21%
Murder[a]	100	95	92	3	5
Sexual Assault[b]	100	79	63	16	21
Robbery	100	87	73	14	13
Aggravated assault	100	72	42	30	28
Other violent[c]	100	73	38	34	27
Property offenses	100%	62%	34%	28%	38%
Burglary	100	71	45	26	29
Larceny[d]	100	63	31	32	37
Fraud[e]	100	50	26	24	50
Drug offenses	100%	72%	35%	37%	28%
Possession	100	70	29	41	30
Trafficking	100	73	39	33	27
Weapons offenses	100%	67%	40%	27%	33%
Other offenses[f]	100%	63%	31%	32%	37%

Note: For persons receiving a combination of sentences, the sentence designation came from the most severe penalty imposed–prison being the most severe, followed by jail, then probation. Prison includes death sentences. Data on sentence type were available for 997,906 cases.

[a]Includes nonnegligent manslaughter.
[b]Includes rape.
[c]Includes offenses such as negligent manslaughter and kidnapping.
[d]Includes motor vehicle theft.
[e]Includes forgery and embezzlement.
[f]Composed of nonviolent offenses such as receiving stolen property and vandalism.

Source: Levin, Langan and Brown (2000).

During recent years, however, states have been redefining the categories of offense that render an offender ineligible for probation—or alternatively, identifying offenders who are low risk and *should* be sentenced to probation. In fact, recent mandatory sentencing laws, such as the popular "three strikes and you're out," have been motivated, in large part, by a desire to limit judicial discretion and the court's ability to grant probation to repeat offenders (Greenwood et al., 1994).

The public perceives that the justice system is too lenient, and when certain statistics are publicized, it appears that way. But, as with other matters involving justice data, the truth is more complicated and it all depends on which populations are included in the summary statistics.

As noted previously in this essay, roughly two-thirds of all adult convicted felons are granted probation. Hence, probation is our nation's most common sentence. Many use this data to characterize U.S. sentencing practices as lenient (Bell and Bennett, 1996). But felony probation terms typically include jail, particularly for person offenses. Levin, Langan, and Brown (2000) reported that overall, 69 percent of convicted felons were sentenced to incarceration in a state prison or local jail, and just 31 percent of were sentenced to straight probation (*see* Table 3).

CHAPTER SIX

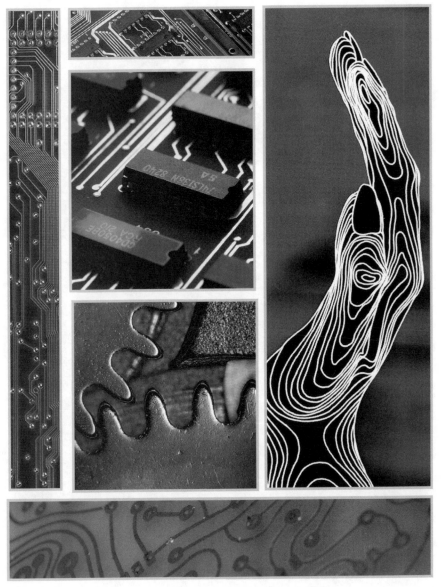

Does Probation Work?

The most common question asked about probation is "does it work?" And, by "work," most mean does the person granted probation refrain from further crime, or reduce his or her *recidivism*. Recidivism is currently the primary outcome measure for probation, as it is for all corrections programs.

Conflicting Reports on Offender Recidivism

Organizations such as the Manhattan Institute's Center for Civic Innovation tend to emphasize the need for probation reform by citing alarming recidivism statistics. For example: one report proclaims almost "two-thirds of probationers commit another crime within three years of their sentence. . . . The roughly 162,000 probationers returned to state prisons and incarcerated in 1991 were responsible for at least 6,400 murders, 7,400 rapes, 10,400 assaults, and 17,000 robberies" (Center for Civic Innovation, 1999:2).

We have no national information on the overall recidivism rates of juvenile probationers, and we only know the "completion rates" for adult misdemeanants. This omission is very important to take note of, since summaries of the effectiveness of probation usually report the recidivism rates of *felons* as if they represented the total of the probation population, and adult felons make up 58 percent of the total probation population (Bonczar, 1997). Failure to make this distinction is why we have profoundly different assessments about whether probation "works."

For example, a review of community corrections by Clear and Braga suggests that adult probation is very successful. They write: "studies show that up to 80 percent of all probationers complete their terms without a new arrest" (1995: 430). But Langan and Cunniff, summarizing data from the same source, conclude: "Within three years of sentencing, while still on probation, 43 percent of these felons were rearrested for a crime within the state. Half of the arrests were for a violent crime (murder, rape, robbery, or aggravated assault) or a drug offense (drug trafficking or drug possession). The estimates (of recidivism) would have been higher had out-of-state arrests been included" (1992: 5).

Reconciling Reports on Offender Recidivism

How can these respected scholars summarize the evidence so differently? The difference is that Clear and Braga are summarizing probation completion rates (not rearrests) for the entire adult felon and misdemeanant population—and most misdemeanants complete probation, whereas Langan and Cunniff are referring to rearrests, and including only adult *felons*—many of whom are rearrested. In most writings on probation effectiveness, the *felon* recidivism rates are presented as representing the entirety of the probation population. Figure 8 shows adult probationer recidivism outcomes, separately for felons versus the entire population.

FIGURE 8: ADULT PROBATION RECIDIVISM OUTCOMES

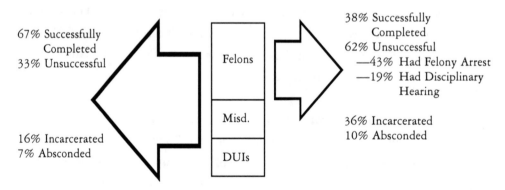

Source: Bureau of Justice Statistics (1992, 1995).

In reality, then, there are two stories to be told in terms of recidivism rates of probationers (similar to the one told above on sentencing practices). On the one hand, recidivism rates are low for the half of the population that is placed on probation for a misdemeanor—data suggest that three-quarters of them successfully complete their supervision. Of course, previous data has shown us that misdemeanants typically receive few services and little supervision, so in essence, they were "rehabilitated" either as a result of their own efforts or simply being placed on probation served some deterrent function and encouraged them to refrain from further crime.

One might then question the wisdom of placing such low-risk persons on probation in the first place, given that probation departments are strapped for funds. Even if one argues that such persons are not receiving direct supervision, there are transactional costs to their being on probation (for example, staff training, administrative costs, office space for files).

More importantly, if these offenders do commit a new crime, probation takes the heat for not providing adequate supervision and perhaps preventing their recidivism. Such bad publicity further tarnishes probation's image. And recently, the practice of not carrying out court-ordered supervision also has served as legal grounds for successfully suing probation departments that failed to adequately supervise offenders who subsequently recidivated (referred to as "negligence in supervision" (for a discussion, *see* del Carmen and Pilant, 1994).

The other story is that for *felons* placed on probation, recidivism rates are high, particularly in jurisdictions that use probation extensively, where there are high risk offenders and where supervision is minimal. In 1985, RAND researchers tracked, for a three-year period, a sample of 1,672 felony probationers sentenced in Los Angeles and Alameda Counties in 1980. Over that time period, the researchers found that 65 percent of the probationers were rearrested, 51 percent were reconvicted, and 34 percent were reincarcerated (Petersilia et al., 1985).

Other agencies replicated the RAND study and the results showed that felony probationer recidivism rates varied greatly from place to place, depending on the seriousness of the underlying population characteristics, the length of follow-up, and the surveillance provided. Geerken and Hayes (1993) summarized seventeen follow-up studies of adult felony probationers and found that felony rearrest rates varied from a low of 12 percent to a high of 65 percent. Such wide variation in recidivism is not unexpected, given the wide variability in granting probation and monitoring court-ordered conditions, as previously discussed.

Predicting Probationer Recidivism

Several research studies have examined probationers' background and criminal record in an attempt to identify those characteristics that are associated with recidivism (for example, Petersilia et al., 1985; Petersilia and Turner, 1993; Langan, 1994). The results are consistent across studies, and Morgan (1993) summarized them as follows:

- *The kind of crime conviction and extent of prior record:* Offenders with more previous convictions and property offenders (burglary as compared to robbery and drug offenders) showed higher rates of recidivism.

- *Income at arrest:* Higher unemployment/lower income are associated with higher recidivism.

- *Household composition:* Persons living with spouse and/or children have lower recidivism.

- *Age:* Younger offenders have higher recidivism rates than older offenders.

- *Drug use:* Probationers who used heroin had higher recidivism rates.

In the Petersilia and Turner (1986) study, these factors were shown to be correlated with recidivism; however, the ability to *predict* recidivism was limited. Knowing this information, and using it to predict which probationers would recidivate and which would not, resulted in accurate predictions only about 70 percent of the time. The authors concluded that the probation programs the offender participated in, along with factors in the environment in which offenders were supervised (family support, employment prospects), predicted recidivism as much or more than the factors present prior to sentencing and often used in recidivism prediction models. Despite the desire to predict offender recidivism, it appears that data and statistical methods are simply insufficient to do so at this time.

Comparing Probationer and Parolee Recidivism

Proponents of probation often argue that although probationer recidivism rates may be unacceptably high, parolee recidivism rates are even higher. To buttress their arguments, they usually compare the recidivism rates of all released prisoners with the recidivism rates of all probationers to show the greater benefits of probation versus prison. Generally—and not surprisingly—the probationers' recidivism rates are lower compared with prisoner recidivism rates. But this conclusion rests on flawed methodology, since there are basic differences between probationers and prisoners, as groups, and these differences certainly influence recidivism.

Petersilia and Turner (1986) conducted a study using a quasi-experimental design that incorporated matching and statistical controls to tease out the issue of comparative recidivism rates. They constructed a sample of 511 prisoners and 511 felony probationers who were comparable in terms of county of conviction, conviction crime, prior criminal record, age, and other characteristics, except that some went to prison while others were placed on felony probation. In the two-year follow-up period, 72 percent of the prisoners were rearrested, as compared with 63 percent of the probationers; 53 percent of the prisoners had new filed charges, compared with 38 percent of the probationers; and 47 percent of the prisoners were incarcerated in jail or prison, compared with 31 percent of the probationers. However, although the prisoners' recidivism rates were higher than the probationers', their new crimes were no more serious, nor was there a significant difference in the length of time before their first filed charge (the average was about six months for both groups).

This study suggests that prison might have made offenders more likely to recidivate than they would have been without the prison experience, although only a randomly designed experiment—where identically matched offenders are randomly assigned to prison versus probation—could confidently conclude that, and as yet, none has ever been conducted.

Other Probation Outcome Measures: Probationers' Contribution to Overall Crime

Another way to examine probation effectiveness is to look at the contribution of those on probation to the overall crime problem. The best measure of this comes from the Bureau of Justice Statistics' *National Pretrial Reporting Program*, which provides data on the pretrial status of persons charged with felonies, collected from a sample which is representative of the seventy-five largest counties in the

FIGURE 9: PERCENT OF FELONY DEFENDENTS ON PROBATION AT THE TIME OF ARREST BY CRIME TYPE, 1996

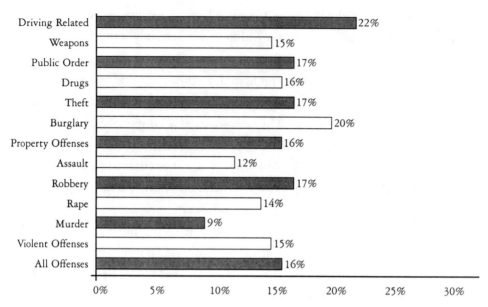

Source: Hart and Reaves (1999).

nation. The most recent Bureau of Justice Statistics data is from 1996 and contained in Hart and Reaves (1999). Figure 9 shows that of all persons arrested and charged with felonies in 1996, 16 percent of them were on probation at the time of their arrest.

From other Bureau of Justice Statistics data, we can determine what percentage of offenders in different status levels were on probation at the time of their arrest (Figure 10). Of those in prison during 1991 (Bureau of Justice Statistics, 1993) and included in the Bureau of Justice Statistics nationally representative *Survey of State Prison Inmates*, 29 percent were on probation at the time of the offense that landed them in prison. The Bureau of Justice Statistics further reports that 31 percent of persons on death row in 1992 reported committing their murders while under probation or parole supervision (Bureau of Justice Statistics, 1994c).

FIGURE 10: PERCENT OF OFFENDERS ON PROBATION OR PAROLE AT THE TIME OF THEIR OFFENSE

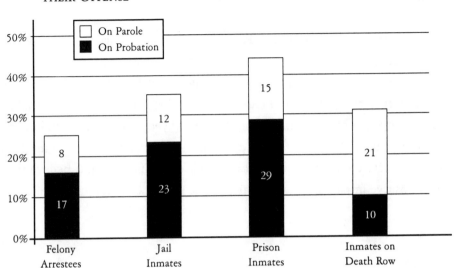

Source: Beck (1991); Bureau of Justice Statistics (1993, 1994a); Reaves and Smith (1995).

Alternative Outcome Measures: Probationer Participation in Treatment and Work Programs

Probation practitioners have expressed concern about the use of recidivism as the primary, if not sole, measure of their program's success (Boone and Fulton, 1995). They note that crime is the result of a long line of social ills—dysfunctional families, economic and educational deprivation, and so on—and these social problems are clearly beyond the direct influence of probation agencies. Moreover, using recidivism as the primary indicator of probation's success fails to reflect the multitude of goals and objectives of probation, and it serves to further erode the public's confidence in probation services, since correctional programs, by and large, have been unable to significantly reduce recidivism.

The American Probation and Parole Association (APPA), the well-respected national association representing U.S. probation officers, has begun to argue persuasively that recidivism rates measure just one function, while ignoring other critical probation tasks, such as preparing presentence investigations, collecting fines and fees, monitoring community service, and so on (Boone and Fulton,

1995). Other scholars have specified how community corrections outcomes might be appropriately measured (Petersilia,1993).

The American Probation and Parole Association has urged its member agencies to collect data on alternative outcomes, such as: amount of restitution collected; number of offenders employed; amount of fines/fees collected; hours of community service; number of treatment sessions; percentage of financial obligation collected; enrollment in school; days employed; educational attainment; and number of days drug-free. Some probation departments have begun to report such alternative outcomes measures to their constituencies and believe it is having a positive impact on staff morale, public image, and funding (Griffin, 1996).

CHAPTER SEVEN

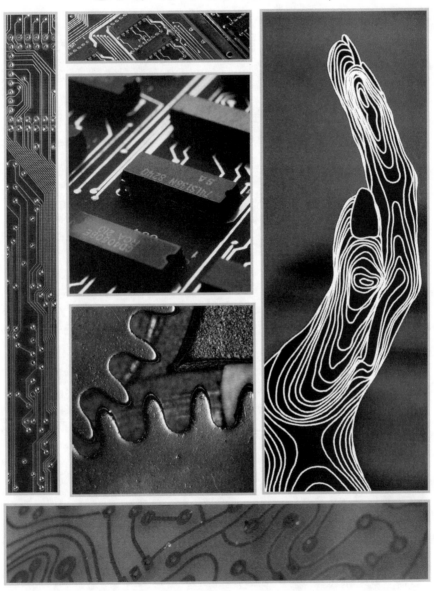

How Can Probation Be Revived?

Probation finds itself in a unique position in the United States. It was originally advanced by liberal reformers, who sought to help offenders overcome their problems and mitigate the perceived harshness of jails and prisons. The public is now less concerned with helping offenders than they are with public safety and deserved punishment. But the public's tough-on-crime stance has caused jail and prison crowding nationwide, and the costs of sending a greater number of convicted offenders to prison has proven prohibitively expensive.

The public has now come to understand that not all criminals can be locked up, and so renewed attention is being focused on probation. Specifically, policy makers are asking whether probation can implement less expensive but more credible and effective community-based sentencing options. No one is advocating the abolition of probation, rather everyone is calling for its reform. But exactly how should we begin?

Implementing Quality Programming for Appropriate Probation Target Groups: "Broken Windows" Community Corrections

One way to start reforming probation is to involve probationers themselves in the reinvention—and provide them an incentive to change. In 1992, New York City's probation department faced a four-year budget cut of $3.3 million. Instead of releasing the cut's equivalent of probation officers (one-third of its corps of 350), the department culled its members into teams and spent more than a year revolutionizing its operations. They redesigned the process of risk assessment; refocused their attention on the most violent offenders; revised their needs assessment plans by focusing on long- and short-term offender goals; and reinvigorated the offender-tracking process through the use of such technology as automated case tracking and computerized kiosks placed citywide. If making the probation process more efficient was insufficient motivation, the administration implemented further incentives: they promised that one-third of the money saved by the new methods would be shared with probation officers in the form of salary, training, or benefits. Several years after the city's probation department instilled the changes, administrators and union leaders alike continued to support them (Linden, 1996).

Another way to start is to mirror successful reforms in other aspects of criminal justice. Within the last ten years, a call has emerged to translate the "broken windows" philosophy of policing into a similar community corrections philosophy. The "broken windows" metaphor is premised on the notion that a community permitting smaller civil disorders leaves itself vulnerable to larger crime. This new community-policing paradigm was embraced by the National Association of Probation Executives (NAPE) and the American Probation and Parole Association (APPA), and by 1999, aspects of "broken window" probation could be seen in cities ranging from Boston to Spokane to Phoenix (Reinventing Probation Council, 1999).

The philosophy is based on community members and organizations (1) teaming up with corrections, (2) placing responsibility squarely on the shoulders of probationers, and (3) aiming first and foremost for public safety. "Broken windows" probation departments, such as those in Boston and Suffolk County (New York), form partnerships with their neighborhoods, health services, businesses, and faith-based organizations to accomplish their goals. To increase probationer responsibility, probation departments in Phoenix's Maricopa County and Tucson's Pima County (Arizona) increase offender contact by working increased, nontraditional hours: this epitomizes the notion that "[w]hile the office is rightly the base of probation supervision, the neighborhood should be the place of supervision" (Reinventing Probation Council, 1999: 5).

To ensure the primary goal of public safety, these probation departments refine other aspects of community policing as well. These include reallocating resources according to risk/needs assessments, putting officers in geographical "place-based supervision" regions to infiltrate the probationers' neighborhoods, and enforcing graduated sanctions such as house arrest, electronic monitoring, and mandatory substance abuse treatment (Reinventing Probation Council, 1999).

"Broken windows" probation has emerged as one important view into the future of community corrections. When the U.S. Department of Justice's Office of Justice Programs gathered national probation and parole leaders for a "strategic discussion" on rethinking probation, they asked those leaders to project possible future goals of community corrections. Participants suggested that, among other goals, community corrections could aim for "public safety," which they envisioned as a community feeling of freedom from danger (as opposed to living in fear to achieve a low crime rate). Their conception of "public safety" and its implications for community corrections mirrors the ideals of "broken windows" probation. Among other implications, they foresaw increasing offender exposure to various social services, tailoring the offenders' supervision to risk/needs assessment, and engaging with the offender in his or her natural environment (Office of Justice Program, 1998).

Implementing Quality Programming for Appropriate Probation Target Groups: Intermediate Sanctions Programs

Helping communities feel they are safe from offenders will go a long way in regaining public trust in probation. However, communities also want assurance that offenders will be punished and that probation will be a meaningful, credible sanction. Beginning in the 1980s, three converging conditions and events spurred the popularity of intermediate sanctions programs (ISPs). First, prison crowding and poor economic conditions crippled corrections departments in the southern United States. Then, a 1986 National Institute of Justice-funded RAND study showed the high recidivism rate of probationers after only three years. Finally, Norval Morris and Michael Tonry released the influential 1990 book *Between Prison and Probation: Intermediate Punishments in a Rational Sentencing System*. This crystallized the argument that intermediate sanctions (based on seriousness of crime) better served victims and justice systems than did indiscriminate imprisonment (Petersilia, 1998).

During the last decade, many jurisdictions developed "intermediate sanctions" (for example, house arrest, electronic monitoring, intensive surveillance, and, to a lesser extent, boot camps) as a response to prison crowding. These programs were designed to be community-based sanctions that were tougher than regular probation, but less stringent and expensive than prison (Gowdy, 1993; Tonry and Lynch, 1996; Clear and Braga, 1995).

Problems with Intermediate Sanctions Programs

The intermediate sanctions program models were good and could have worked, except for two critical factors. First, they usually were implemented without creating an organizational capacity to ensure compliance with the court-ordered conditions (*see* Parent et al., 1997). Intermediate sanctions were designed for smaller caseloads enabling officers to provide both services and monitoring for new criminal activity. For example: a well-publicized Georgia program teamed two probation officers per twenty-five offenders, a ratio far lower than most systems can maintain. But many others were never given the resources needed to enforce the sanctions or provide necessary treatment.

When the court ordered offenders to participate in drug treatment, for example, many probation officers could not ensure compliance because local treatment programs were unavailable (Turner et al., 1994). Programs that were available often put offenders at the back of the waiting list. Similarly, when the court-ordered fines or restitution to be paid, or community service to be performed, it often was ignored because of a lack of personnel to follow-through and monitor such requirements (Petersilia and Turner, 1993).

Secondly, it became clear by the late 1990s that relatively few offenders participated in intermediate sanction programs. In 1997, virtually every state (as well as the federal government) reported having intermediate sanctions programs, but fewer than 6 percent of the almost three million adult probationers and parolees in the United States were estimated to be participating in them

(Camp and Camp, 1997). All fifty states have reported using electronic monitoring; however, its use with probationers and parolees has peaked at 1 percent (Camp and Camp, 2000). Although thirty-five states have reported operating boot camps, the combined daily census has never exceeded 10,000 participants; a mere 5,800 probationers completed boot camps in 1998. Finally, nearly 125 day reporting centers operate in the United States, but their combined daily population is less than 15,000 (Camp and Camp, 1999; Parent et al, 1995). An estimated 10 percent of adult probationers and parolees participate in intermediate sanctions programs. However, the programs have not involved the bulk of offenders for whom they would be most appropriate: ex-felon probationers with serious prior records and a history of substance abuse (Petersilia, 1998).

Over time, what was intended as tougher community corrections in most jurisdictions did not materialize, thereby further tarnishing probation's image. As Andrew Klein, former chief probation officer in Quincy, Massachusetts (1997:311) so eloquently put it:

> Unenforced sanctions jeopardize any sentence, undermining its credibility and potential to address serious sentencing concerns . . . they are like sentences to prison with cell doors that do not lock and perimeter gates that slip open. The moment the word gets out that the alternative sentence or intermediate sanction is unmonitored is the moment the court loses another sentencing option.

Ironically, another downfall of intermediate sanctions programs has been its success at supervising probationers. Intermediate sanction program supervision did not decrease subsequent arrests nor overall justice system costs. However, technical violations by their participating probationers increased. According to Petersilia and Turner (1993), whose intermediate sanctions programs national demonstration-evaluation involved fourteen counties in nine states, intermediate sanctions program offenders had relatively the same number of subsequent arrests, but more technical violations and returns to incarceration, than their non-intermediate sanction program counterparts. Because close surveillance probably uncovered more technical violations—and because it is unlikely intermediate sanction program offenders actually committed more violations—the notion that intermediate sanctions and increased surveillance would act as crime deterrents became questionable (Petersilia, 1998).

While most judges still report being anxious to use tougher, community-based programs as alternatives to routine probation or prison, most are skeptical that the programs promised "on paper" actually will be delivered in practice (Sigler and Lamb, 1994). As a result, some intermediate sanction programs are beginning to fall into disuse (Petersilia, 1995b).

Successful Intermediate Sanctions Programs

However, not all intermediate sanctions programs have had this experience. In a few instances, communities invested in intermediate sanctions and made the necessary treatment and work programs available to offenders (Klein, 1997). And, most importantly, the programs worked: in programs where offenders received *both* surveillance (for example, drug tests) and participated in relevant treatment, recidivism was reduced 20 to 30 percent (Petersilia and Turner, 1993). More recent program evaluations in Texas, Wisconsin, Oregon, and Colorado have found similarly encouraging results (Clear and Braga, 1995). Even the national Bureau of Justice Statistics probation follow-up study by Langan (1994) found that if probationers were participating in or making progress in treatment programs, they were less likely to have a new arrest (38 percent) than either those drug offenders who had made no progress (66 percent) or those who were not ordered to be tested or treated (48 percent).

There now exists rather solid empirical evidence that ordering offenders into treatment, and getting them to participate, reduces recidivism (Gendreau, 1996; Anglin and Hser, 1990; Lipton, 1995; Latessa, 1999). Even some boot camps (which traditionally relied solely on physical, militaristic tactics) are now enhancing their therapeutic programs (Petersilia, 1998). So, the first order of business must be to allocate sufficient resources so that the designed programs (incorporating both surveillance and treatment) can be implemented. Sufficient monetary resources are essential to obtaining and sustaining judicial support, and achieving program success.

Public Perception of Intermediate Sanctions Programs

Quality probation supervision costs money, and we should be honest about that. We currently spend about $700 to $3,500 per year, per probationer for supervision; home confinement supervision plus electronic monitoring costs more than $6,500 annually (Camp and Camp, 2000; Gowen, 2000). Even in our richer probation departments, the annual dollars spent on probation supervision is well below $1,000 per probationer (Abadinsky, 1997). It is no wonder that recidivism rates are so high. Effective substance abuse treatment programs are estimated to cost at least $12,000 to $14,000 per year (Lipton, 1995). Those resources will be forthcoming only if the public believes the programs are both effective and punitive.

Public opinion often is cited by officials as the reason for supporting expanded prison policies. According to officials, the public demands a "get tough on crime" policy, which is synonymous with sending more offenders to prison for longer terms (Bell and Bennett, 1996). We must publicize recent evidence showing that offenders—whose opinion on such matters is critical for deterrence—judge some intermediate sanctions as more punishing than prison. Surveys of offenders in Minnesota, Arizona, New Jersey, Oregon, and Texas reveal that when offenders are asked to equate criminal sentences, they judge certain types of community punishments as more severe than prison (Crouch, 1993; Petersilia and Deschenes, 1994; Spelman, 1995; Wood and Grasmick, 1995).

One of the more striking examples comes from Marion County, Oregon. Selected nonviolent offenders were given the choice of serving a prison term or returning to the community to participate in the Intensive Supervision Probation program, which imposed drug testing, mandatory community service, and frequent visits with the probation officer. About a third of the offenders given the option between Intensive Supervision Probation or prison chose prison. When Minnesota inmates and corrections staff were asked to equate a variety of criminal sentences, they rated three years of intensive supervision probation as equivalent in punitiveness to one year in prison (Petersilia and Deschenes, 1994).

Imprisonment Versus Intermediate Sanctions Programs

What accounts for this seeming aberration? Why should anyone prefer imprisonment to remaining in the community—no matter what the conditions? Some have suggested that prison has lost some of its punitive sting, and hence its ability to scare and deter. For one, possessing a prison record is not as stigmatizing as in the past, because so many of the offender's peers (and family members) also have "done time." Further, about a quarter of all U.S. black males will be incarcerated during their lives, so the stigma attached to having a prison record is not as great as it was when it was relatively uncommon (Mauer and Huling, 1995). And the pains associated with prison—social isolation, fear of victimization—seem less severe for repeat offenders who have learned how to do time.

In fact, far from stigmatizing, prison evidently confers status in some neighborhoods. Jerome Skolnick of the University of California-Berkeley found that for drug dealers in California, imprisonment confers a certain elevated "home boy" status, especially for gang members for whom prison and prison gangs can be an alternative site of loyalty (Skolnick, 1990). And according to the California Youth Authority, inmates steal state-issued prison clothing for the same reason. Wearing it when they return to the community lets everyone know they have done "hard time" (Petersilia, 1992).

The length of time an offender can be expected to serve in prison also has decreased. The latest statistics show that the average U.S. prison term for those released to parole is seventeen months (Maquire and Pastore, 1995). But more to the point, for less serious offenders, the expected time served can be much less. In California, for example, more than half of all offenders entering prison in 1990 were expected to serve six months or less (Petersilia, 1992). Offenders on the street may be aware of this, perhaps because of the extensive media coverage such issues receive.

For convicted felons, freedom, of course, is preferable to prison. But the type of probation program being advocated here—combining heavy doses of surveillance and treatment—does not represent freedom. In fact, as suggested above, such community-based programs may have a more punitive bite than prison.

Consider a comparison between Contra Costa (California) County's Intensive Supervision Program for drug offenders, which was discontinued in 1990 due to a shortage of funds, with what drug offenders would face if imprisoned:

- *Intensive Supervision Program.* Offenders are required to serve at least one year in the Intensive Supervision Program. In addition to twice weekly face-to-face contacts, the Intensive Supervision Program includes a random drug testing hotline, Saturday home visits, weekly Narcotics Anonymous meetings, special assistance from police to expedite existing bench warrants, a liaison with the State Employment Development Department. To remain on the Intensive Supervision Program, offenders must be employed or in treatment, perform community service, pay victim restitution, and remain crime and drug-free.

- *Prison.* A sentence of twelve months will require that offenders serve about half of that. During their term, they are not required to work nor will they be required to participate in any training or treatment, but they may do so if they wish. Once released, they probably will be placed on routine parole supervision, where they might see their officer once a month.

It is important to publicize these results, particularly to policymakers, who say they are imprisoning such a large number of offenders because of the public's desire to get tough on crime. But it is no longer necessary to equate criminal punishment solely with imprisonment. The balance of sanctions between probation and prison can be shifted, and at some level of intensity and length, intermediate punishments can be the more dreaded penalty.

Appropriate Probation Target Groups: Drug Offenders

Once the support and organizational capacity is in place, we need to target the offender group that makes the most sense, given our current state of knowledge regarding program effectiveness (for a review, *see* Harland, 1996). Targeting drug offenders makes the most sense for a number of reasons. Drug offenders were not always punished so frequently by imprisonment. In California, for example, just 5 percent of convicted drug offenders were sentenced to prison in 1980, but by 1990 the number had increased to 20 percent (Petersilia,1992). The large scale imprisonment of drug offenders has taken place only recently, and there is some new evidence suggesting that the public seems ready to shift their punishment strategies for low-level drug offenders.

A 1994 nationwide poll by Hart Research Associates reported that Americans have come to understand that drug abuse is not simply a failure of willpower or a violation of criminal law (Peter D. Hart Associates, Inc., 1994). They now see the problem as far more complex, involving not only individual behavior but also fundamental issues of poverty, opportunity, and personal circumstances. The Drug Strategies report (Falco, 1995) reports that nearly half of all Americans have been touched directly by the drug problem: 45 percent of those surveyed in the 1994 Hart poll said that they knew someone who became addicted to a drug other than alcohol (Peter D. Hart Associates, Inc., 1994). This personal knowledge is changing attitudes about how to deal with the problem: seven in ten believe that their addicted acquaintance would have been helped more by entering a supervised treatment program than by being sentenced to prison.

It appears that the public now wants tougher sentences for drug traffickers and more treatment for addicts—what legislators have instead given them are long sentences for everyone. The Drug Strategies group, who analyzed the Hart survey, concluded that "Public opinion on drugs is more pragmatic and less ideological than the current political debate reflects. Voters know that punitive approaches won't work" (Falco, 1995).

Another recent national telephone survey confirms these findings (Flanagan and Longmire, 1996). They concluded that: 1) respondents favored treatment rather than punishment as the best alternative to reduce the use of illegal drugs, and 2) Americans want to see a change in drug control strategy (Cintron and Johnson, 1996) The public receptiveness to treatment for addicts is important, because those familiar with delivering treatment say that is where treatment can make the biggest impact.

A report by the prestigious Institute of Medicine (1990) recommends focusing on probationers and parolees to curb drug use and related crime. They noted that about one-fifth of the estimated population needing treatment—and two-fifths of those clearly needing it—are under the supervision of the justice system as parolees or probationers. And since the largest single group of serious drug users in any locality comes through the justice system every day, the report concludes that the justice system is one of the most important gateways to treatment delivery and we should be using it more effectively.

Moreover, research has shown that those under corrections supervision stay in treatment longer, thereby increasing positive treatment outcomes. The claim that individuals forced into treatment by the courts will not be successful has not been borne out by research. In fact, just the opposite is true. Research at the University of California Los Angeles and elsewhere has provided strong evidence not only that drug abuse treatment is effective, but also that individuals coerced into treatment derive as many benefits as those who enter voluntarily (Anglin and Hser, 1990; Latessa, 1999).

The largest study of drug treatment outcomes found that justice system clients stayed in treatment longer than clients with no justice system involvement, and as a result, had higher than average success rates (Institute of Medicine, 1990). The evidence suggests that drug treatment is effective for both men and women, Anglos, and minority ethnic groups, young and old, and criminal and noncriminal participants.

However, as noted above, quality treatment does not come cheap. But in terms of crime and health costs averted, it is an investment that pays for itself immediately. Researchers in California recently conducted an assessment of drug treatment programs, and identified those that were successful, concluding that it now can be "documented that treatment and recovery programs are a good investment" (Gerstein, et al., 1994). The researchers studied a sample of 1,900 treatment participants, followed them up for as much as two years of treatment, and studied participants from all four major treatment modalities (therapeutic communities, social models, outpatient drug free, and methadone maintenance). Gerstein et al. (1994:33) conclude:

- Treatment was very cost beneficial: for every dollar spent on drug and alcohol treatment, the State of California saved $7 in reductions in crime and health care costs. The study found that each day of treatment *paid for itself on the day treatment was received*, primarily through an avoidance of crime.

- The level of criminal activity declined by two-thirds from before treatment to after treatment. The greater the length of time spent in treatment, the greater the reduction in crime. Reported criminal activity declined before and after treatment as follows: mean number of times sold or helped sell drugs (-75 percent), mean number of times weapon/physical force used (-93 percent), percent committing any illegal activity (-72 percent), and mean months involved in criminal activity (-80 percent).

Regardless of the type of treatment modality, reduction in crime was substantial and significant (although participants in the social model recovery programs had the biggest reduction). In the California study, the most effective treatment programs cost about $12,000 per year, per client (Gerstein et al., 1994). University of California Los Angeles researchers recently concluded: "It seems that drug abuse treatment mandated by the criminal justice system represents one of the best and most cost-effective approaches to breaking the pernicious cycle of drug use, criminality, incarceration, and recidivism" (Prendergast, Anglin, and Wellisch, 1995).

Implementing Quality Programming for Appropriate Target Groups: Summary

In sum, there are several steps to achieving greater crime control over probationers and parolees. First, we must provide adequate financial resources to deliver programs that have been shown to work. Successful programs combine *both* treatment and surveillance, and are targeted toward appropriate offender subgroups. Current evidence suggests low-level drug offenders are prime candidates for the intermediate sanction programs considered here. Then, we must garner support, convincing the public that the probation sanction is punitive, and convincing the judiciary that offenders will be held accountable for their behavior.

Of course, there is much more to reforming the probation system than simply targeting low-level drug offenders for effective treatment, but this would be a start. We also need to seriously reconsider probation's underlying mission, administrative structure, and funding base. And, we need to fund a program of basic research to address some of probation's most pressing problems.

Make Probation a Priority Research Topic

Basic research on probation has diminished in recent years, except for the evaluations funded by the National Institute of Justice on intermediate sanctions. While these early evaluations are instructive, their results are by no means definitive. The programs mostly have been surveillance-oriented, and have focused primarily on increasing drug testing and face-to-face contacts with offenders. They have incorporated little treatment or employment training. Most intermediate sanction programs targeted serious career criminals, with lengthy histories of crime and substance abuse.

As noted in this chapter, there is some supportive evidence that intermediate sanctions incorporating treatment, in addition to surveillance activities, do produce lower recidivism. It is also possible that had these programs been targeted toward less serious offenders, or earlier in their criminal careers, the results might have been more encouraging. There is reason to continue experimenting with community-based sanctions, and varying target populations, program elements, setting, and point in their criminal career for intervention.

Researching Community Supervision

Technical violations in community supervision are an important consideration for probation researchers. Probation and parole officers spend most of their time monitoring the technical conditions imposed by the courts (such as no alcohol or drug use). When violations are discovered, additional time is spent in processing the paperwork necessary to revoke offenders. Many of those offenders are revoked to prison, most of them for violations of the "no drug use" condition, as detected through urine testing. Such revocations undoubtedly will increase as urinalysis testing for drugs becomes less expensive and more widespread.

This begs two important research questions: what purpose is served by monitoring and revoking persons for technical violations, and is the benefit worth the cost? If technical violations identify offenders who are "going bad" and likely to commit crime, then we may wish to spend the time uncovering such conditions and incarcerating those persons. On the other hand, if technical violators are simply troubled, but not criminally dangerous, then devoting our scarce prison resources to this population might not be warranted. Despite the policy significance of technical violations, little serious research has focused on this issue. As the costs of monitoring and incarcerating technical violators increases, research must examine its crime control significance.

Researching Prison Populations

There is also the ongoing debate about who is in prison, and whether there exists a group of prisoners who, based on crime and prior criminal records, safely could be supervised in the community. Proponents of alternatives argue that over the past decade, we have vastly expanded the use of imprisonment, and as a result many low-level offenders have gotten caught up in the broader net of social control, and are now in prison. They contend that many (if not most) prisoners are minor property offenders, low-level drug dealers, or technical violators—ideal candidates for community based alternatives. Those who are against expanding prison alternatives disagree, citing data showing that most prisoners are violent recidivists with few prospects for reform.

It is likely that the truth lies somewhere in between, and that the differences in the numbers cited depend on how one aggregates the data, and what data set one chooses to analyze. It is likely that historical sentencing patterns have resulted in vastly different populations being incarcerated in different states. Research examining the characteristics of inmates in different states (by age, criminal record, and substance abuse history) is necessary to clarify this important debate. It is also critical that we conduct better follow-up studies (ideally, using experimental designs) of offenders who have been sentenced to prison as opposed to those in various forms of community supervision. By tracking similarly situated offenders, sentenced differently, we will be able to refine our recidivism-prediction models and begin to estimate more accurately the crime and cost implications of different sentencing models.

Researching Criminal Justice Agencies

We also need to move away from the fragmentary studies of individual agencies and toward a more comprehensive assessment of how probation departments and other justice agencies influence one another and together influence crime. Decisions made in one justice agency have dramatic workload and cost implications for other justice agencies, and later decisions (such as the probation policy on violating technical provisions). To date, these systematic effects have not been well studied, and much benefit is likely to come from examining how various policy initiatives affect criminal justice agencies, individually and collectively. Generating more arrests will not necessarily result in more convictions and incarcerations if prosecutors and corrections (either by policy or budget constraints) do not follow through with convictions and incarcerations. Many past probation reforms—implemented by well-meaning probation staff—have been negated by the failure of other justice system agencies to cooperate in the program.

The issues presented are only a few of the salient themes that should be pursued to better understand the nation's probation system. Probation has much untapped potential, and with research and program attention, can become an integral part of our nation's fight against crime.

QUESTIONS AND ANSWERS

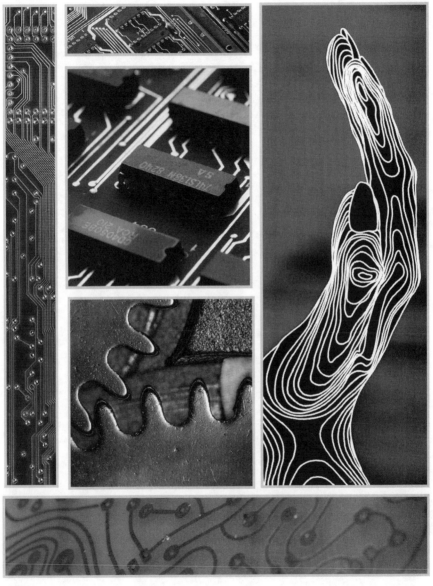

Probation and Intermediate Sanctions in the United States

Multiple Choice Questions

Circle the letter of the correct answer.

1. Probation is defined as:
   a. A court-ordered disposition in lieu of imprisonment
   b. A combined jail and community service sentence
   c. A sentence that mandates community service requirements
   d. A sentence reached through plea-bargaining

2. What was the first state to adopt and legalize probation?
   a. California
   b. Ohio
   c. Massachusetts
   d. Minnesota

3. Which criminal justice agency is most comprehensively involved with criminal offenders?
   a. Police
   b. Probation
   c. Prosecutors
   d. Parole board members

4. Probation was originally intended for:
   a. First-time offenders
   b. Elderly offenders
   c. Indigent offenders
   d. Drug offenders

5. What is regarded as the major outcome measure of probation?
   a. Amount of fines collected
   b. Amount of community service performed
   c. Recidivism
   d. Extent of participation in treatment programs

6. Probationers make up _____ of all U.S. adults under correctional supervision.
   a. 25 percent
   b. 40 percent
   c. 60 percent
   d. 90 percent

7. Whenever a probationer fails to comply with the specified conditions of his or her probation, other than committing a new crime, a _____ is said to have occurred.
   a. Serious violation
   b. Mandatory violation
   c. Technical violation
   d. Supervisory violation

8. This person is generally recognized as the world's first probation officer:
   a. John Crofton
   b. John Maconochie
   c. John Augustus
   d. John Brockway

9. The most frequently applied criminal sanction in the United States is_____.
   a. Parole
   b. Prison
   c. Probation
   d. House arrest

10. Punishments that are less severe and costly than prison but more restrictive than traditional probation are called:
    a. Restorative sanctions
    b. Indeterminate sanctions
    c. Intermediate sanctions
    d. Immediate sanctions

11. It is well known that probation departments serve which two dual functions?
    a. Supervision and investigation
    b. Surveillance and enforcement
    c. Drug testing and investigating crimes
    d. Law enforcement and victim services

12. A sanction in which an offender is sentenced to probation plus a term of incarceration in jail or prison is known as:
    a. Split sentencing
    b. Indeterminate sentencing
    c. Modification of sentence
    d. Intermittent incarceration

13. Probation is basically a contract between the offender and the:
    a. Warden
    b. Probation board
    c. District attorney
    d. Judge

14. The requirements to report once a month to a probation officer and notify his or her office about any change of address are examples of:
    a. Standard conditions
    b. Treatment conditions
    c. Punitive conditions
    d. Restorative justice conditions

15. An investigation and summary report of the background of a convicted offender, prepared to help the judge decide on an appropriate sentence, is known as:
    a. Background summation report
    b. Presentence report
    c. Probation guidelines report
    d. Sentencing guidelines report

16. Petersilia and Turner's national evaluation of intensive supervision probation (ISP) found the following:
    a. Offenders commit a large number of violent crimes within the first month
    b. Large numbers of rule violations are found
    c. Significant costs savings are found
    d. Law enforcement officials dislike the program

17. The most common condition placed on probationers in the United States is:
    a. House arrest
    b. Electronic monitoring
    c. Drug testing
    d. Participation in substance abuse treatment

18. Increasing numbers of felons are being sentenced to probation and intermediate sanctions because:
    a. Judges are too soft on crime
    b. The rehabilitation model has emerged
    c. It is required by the Supreme Court
    d. Prisons are crowded and expensive

19. During the late 1970s and early 1980s, probation developed an orientation toward:
    a. Greater rehabilitation services for offenders
    b. Greater supervision of offenders
    c. Greater advocacy on behalf of offenders
    d. Smaller caseloads

20. Generally, states with a relatively high per capita imprisonment rate:
    a. Also have a relatively high per capita use of probation
    b. Have a relatively low per capita use of probation
    c. Do not use probation
    d. Have relatively low recidivism rates

21. Petersilia and Turner's national evaluation of intensive supervision programs (ISP) showed that when participating offenders received both surveillance (such as drug testing) and relevant treatment, their recidivism rates:
    a. Were reduced by 20 to 30 percent
    b. Were increased by 50 to 75 percent
    c. Remained unchanged
    d. The evaluation did not look at this issue

22. The state whose model of intensive supervision probation (ISP) was most influential was_____.
    a. Texas
    b. California
    c. Georgia
    d. Massachusetts

23. Prison populations in the United States have increased in recent years, and probation populations have:
    a. Decreased
    b. Increased
    c. Stayed the same
    d. No data on this exists

24. Current evidence suggests that _____ are prime candidates for enhanced or intensive probation programs.
    a. Low-level drug offenders
    b. Sex offenders
    c. Property offenders
    d. Elderly criminals

25. Nationally, what percentage of the correctional budget is devoted to supervising offenders in the community?
    a. 10 percent
    b. 30 percent
    c. 50 percent
    d. 75 percent

Short Essay Questions:

Answer the following in complete sentences.

1. Explain why anyone would prefer prison to probation.
2. Describe the various stages at which probation is involved in the criminal justice process.
3. What criminal characteristics increase the likelihood of recidivism?
4. Why have intermediate sanctions been so quickly and extensively adopted throughout corrections?
5. According to the text, what are the advantages and disadvantages of probation (compared to incarceration)?
6. How did probation develop in America?

Multiple Choice Answers:

1. a.	14. a.
2. c.	15. b.
3. b.	16. b.
4. a.	17. c.
5. c.	18. d.
6. c.	19. b.
7. c.	20. a.
8. c.	21. a.
9. c.	22. c.
10. c.	23. b.
11. a.	24. a.
12. a.	25. a.
13. d.	

Short Essay Answers:

1. **Explain why anyone would prefer prison to probation.**

Probation is usually seen by the public and offenders as more lenient than a prison term. But stricter probation sentences, such as those requiring house arrest, electronic monitoring, employment, or drug testing may be quite severe. Also, since offenders usually serve just half of their court-imposed prison sentence (often less than six months), their prison sentence will likely be shorter than their felony probation sentence, which will usually run two-to-three years. So, a shorter term in prison may actually be seen as less harsh in the offender's mind than a longer probation sentence with stringent restrictions. This is particularly true for offenders who have been in prison before, and know how to "do time." In fact, studies done in Texas and Oregon showed that when offenders are given the choice, many prefer a short prison term over a more lengthy intensive probation sentence.

2. **Describe the various stages at which probation is involved in the criminal justice process.**

Probation officials are involved in decision making long before sentencing, often beginning from the point of a crime being noted by the police. They usually perform the personal investigation to determine whether a defendant will be released on his or her own recognizance or bail. Presentence reports, usually prepared by probation officers, are the primary sources of information the court uses to determine which cases will be deferred from formal prosecution. If deferred, probation officers also will supervise the diverted offender and their recommendation will be primary in whether or not the offender has successfully complied with the diversionary sentence. If so, no formal prosecution will occur.

For persons who violate court-ordered conditions, probation officers are responsible for deciding which violations will be brought back to the courts attention, and what subsequent sanctions to recommend. When the court grants probation, probation staff have great discretion about which court-ordered conditions to enforce and monitor. And even when an offender goes to prison, the offender's initial security classification (and eligibility for parole) will be based on information contained in the presentence investigation. Finally, when the offender is released from jail or prison, probation staff often provide his or her community supervision.

3. **What criminal characteristics increase the likelihood of recidivism?**

Research has shown the following characteristics to be associated with recidivism:

- The kind of crime conviction and extent of prior record: offenders with more previous convictions and property offenders (burglary as compared to robbery and drug offenders) showed higher rates of recidivism;
- Income at arrest: higher unemployment and lower income are associated with higher recidivism;
- Household composition: persons living with spouse and/or children have lower recidivism;
- Age: younger offenders have higher recidivism rates than older offenders;
- Drug use: probationers who used heroin and other drugs had higher recidivism rates.

4. **Why have intermediate sanctions been so quickly and extensively adopted throughout corrections?**

Prisons are increasingly expensive and the public is demanding harsh punishment for convicted felons. Most citizens do not believe that probation represents sufficient punishment for serious crimes, and hence the interest in developing something between prison and regular probation. Intermediate sanctions fill this void. Intermediate sanctions represent a variety of programs that can be matched with the offender's risk and needs. For example, if an offender abuses drugs, he can be placed on house arrest, mandated to go to drug treatment, and participate in random drug testing. This intermediate sanction program is less expensive than prison, and in the long run, may do more to help the offender. Also, since offenders remain in the community, they pay taxes, can help support their family, and are not exposed to the criminogenic effects of prison. Finally, if intermediate sanctions incorporate both surveillance and treatment activities, a reduction in recidivism can be expected.

5. **According to the text, what are the advantages and disadvantages of probation (compared to incarceration)?**

Advantages:
- Community corrections aim at building ties that can reintegrate the offender into the community.

- The offender can participate in substance abuse programming, vocational and employment training, and other treatment and work programs.
- The offender can pay back the victim and the community directly through victim restitution and community service.
- The offender's background characteristics or crimes are not serious enough to warrant incarceration.
- Probation is cheaper than incarceration.
- If rehabilitation is measured by recidivism rates, prison is no more effective than probation. In fact, some studies show that just being in prison raises the offender's potential for recidivism. Many believe prisons are "schools for crime," and result in increases in the offender's commitment to criminal lifestyles.
- Family members also suffer if the offender was contributing to the financial support of children and others.

Disadvantages:
- The offender may continue to commit crime, thereby jeopardizing public safety and creating new victims.
- Family members and children may continue to be negatively influenced by the offender's presence (if, for instance, he or she is abusive).
- Victims may feel that probation was a "slap on the wrist" and trivialized their crime.
- If the offenders are rearrested, the system incurs the costs of processing their new case as well as their subsequent incarceration.

6. **How did probation develop in America?**

Probation in the United States began in 1841 with the innovative work of John Augustus, a Boston bootmaker who was the first to post bail for a man charged with being a common drunk. Mr. Augustus was a religious man of financial means, and had some experience working with alcoholics. When the man appeared before the judge for sentencing, Mr. Augustus asked the judge to defer sentencing for three weeks and release the man into his custody. At the end of this brief probationary period, the offender convinced the judge of his reform and therefore received a nominal fine. The concept of probation had been born. During the next fifteen years, Augustus bailed out more than 1,800 persons in the Boston courts. He provided his charges with aid in obtaining employment, an education, or a place to live, and also made an impartial report to the court. Buoyed by Augustus' example, Massachusetts quickly adopted probation for juvenile offenders, and was the first state to formally adopt a probation law for juveniles. Public support for adult probation was much more difficult to come by. It was not until 1901 that New York passed the first statute authorizing probation for adult offenders. By 1956, all states had adopted adult and juvenile probation laws.

Initially, probation officers were volunteers. Early probation volunteer officers were often drawn from church groups. In addition, police were reassigned to function as probation officers while continuing to draw their pay as municipal employees. But as the concept spread and the number of persons arrested increased, the need for presentence investigations and other court investigations increased, and the volunteer probation officer was converted into a paid position. The new officers hired were drawn largely from the law enforcement community and worked directly for the judge. Tasks were continually added to probation's responsibilities, while funding remained constant or declined.

In recent years, probation agencies with meager resources have struggled to upgrade services and supervision. Important developments have included the widespread adoption of case classification systems and various types of intermediate sanctions (such as electronic monitoring or intensive supervision). These programs have had varied success in reducing recidivism, and the debate over the usefulness of probation continues today.

PART I REFERENCES

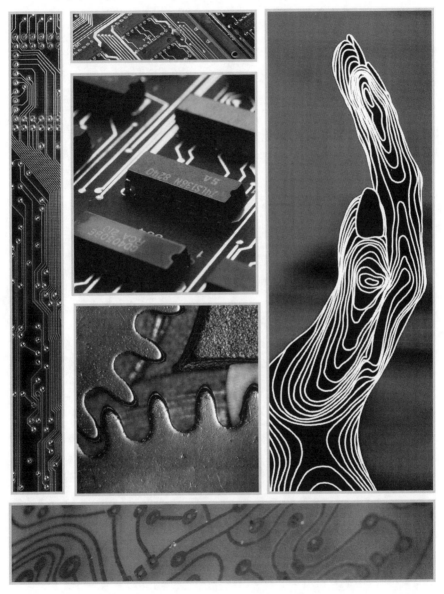

Abadinsky, Howard. 1997. *Probation and Parole: Theory and Practice.* New Jersey: Prentice Hall.

Allen, Harry, Eric W. Carlson, and Evalyn C. Parks. 1979. *Critical Issues in Adult Probation.* National Institute of Law Enforcement and Criminal Justice. Washington, D.C.: U.S. Department of Justice.

American Bar Association. 1970. *Standards Relating to Probation.* Chicago: American Bar Association.

American Correctional Association. 1998. *Dictionary of Criminal Justice Terms.* Lanham, Maryland: American Correctional Association.

———. 2000. *Vital Statistics in Corrections.* Lanham, Maryland: American Correctional Association.

———. 2001a. *Probation and Parole Directory, 2001-2003.* Lanham, Maryland: American Correctional Association.

American Justice Institute. 1981. *Presentence Investigation Report Program.* Sacramento, California: American Justice Institute.

Anglin, Michael and Ying Hser. 1990. "Legal Coercion and Drug Abuse Treatment: Research Findings and Social Policy Implications." In J. A. Inciardi, ed. *Handbook of Drug Control in the United States.* Westport, Connecticut: Greenwood Press. 151-176.

Associated Press. 2001. "Rhode Island Probation System in Crisis." *Boston Globe*, March 6.

Augustus, John. 1939. *A Report of the Labors of John Augustus, for the Last Ten Years, in Aid of the Unfortunate.* Boston: Wright and Hasty. Reprinted as *John Augustus, First Probation Officer.* New York Probation Association.

Baird, Chris, Doug Holien, and Judith Bakke. 1986. *Fees for Probation Services.* Washington, D.C.: U.S. Department of Justice, National Institute of Corrections.

Baird, Christopher, Dennis Wagner, and Robert DeComo. 1995. *Evaluation of the Impact of Oregon's Structured Sanctions Program*. San Francisco: National Council on Crime and Delinquency.

Bearden v. Georgia, 461 U.S. 660 (1983).

Beck, Allen J. 2000. *Prisoners in 1999*. Washington, D.C.: U. S. Department of Justice, Bureau of Justice Statistics.

Beck, Allen and Bernard Shipley. 1989. *Recidivism of Prisoners Released in 1983*. Washington, D.C.: U.S. Department of Justice, Bureau of Justice Statistics.

Begasse, Jen Kiki. 1995. "Oregonians Support Alternatives for Nonviolent Offenders." *Overcrowded Times*. 1, 11-14.

Belenko, Steven. 1998. "Research on Drug Courts: A Critical Review." *National Drug Court Institute Review*.1(1).

Bell, Griffin B. and William J. Bennett. 1996. *The State of Violent Crime in America*. Washington, D.C.: The Council on Crime in America.

Bonczar, Thomas P. 1997. *Characteristics of Adults on Probation, 1995*. Washington, D.C.: U.S. Department of Justice, Bureau of Justice Statistics.

Bonczar, Thomas P. and Lauren E. Glaze. 1999. "Probation and Parole in the United States, 1998." Washington, D.C.: U.S. Department of Justice, Bureau of Justice Statistics.

Boone, Harry N. and Betsy A. Fulton. 1995. *Results-Driven Management: Implementing Performance-Based Measures in Community Corrections*. Lexington, Kentucky: American Probation and Parole Association.

Bork, Michael V. 1995. "Five Year Review of United States Probation Data, 1990-94." *Federal Probation*. 59:4: 27-33.

Bureau of Justice Assistance. 1996. *National Assessment of Structured Sentencing*. Washington, D.C.: U.S. Department of Justice, Bureau of Justice Assistance.

Bureau of Justice Statistics. Unpublished. *Census of Probation and Parole, 1991*. Washington D.C.: U.S. Department of Justice, Bureau of Justice Statistics.

————. 1992. *Census of Probation and Parole, 1991*. Washington, D.C.: U.S. Department of Justice, Bureau of Justice Statistics.

————. 1993. *Survey of State Prison Inmates, 1991*. Washington, D.C.: U.S. Government Printing Office.

————. 1994a. *Probation and Parole, 1991.* Washington, D.C.: U.S. Government Printing Office.

————. 1994b. *Jail Inmates, 1992.* Washington, D.C.: U.S. Government Printing Office.

————. 1994c. *Capital Punishment, 1993.* Washington, D.C.: U.S. Government Printing Office.

————. 1995. *Correctional Populations in the United States, 1992.* Washington, D.C.: U.S. Department of Justice, Bureau of Justice Statistics.

————. 1996. *Correctional Populations in the United States, 1995.* Washington, D.C.: U.S. Department of Justice, Bureau of Justice Statistics.

————. 2000a. *Correctional Populations in the United States, 1997.* Washington, D.C.: U.S. Department of Justice, Bureau of Justice Statistics.

————. 2000b. "U.S. Correctional Population Reaches 6.3 Million Men and Women: Represents 3.1 Percent of the Adult U. S. Population." Press Release. U.S. Department of Justice. June 30.

————. 2001. *Federal Criminal Case Processing, 1999: With Trends, 1982-99.* Washington, D.C.: U.S. Department of Justice, Bureau of Justice Statistics.

California Commission. 1990. *California Blue Ribbon Commission on Inmate Population Management.* Final Report. Sacramento, California.

California Department of Justice, Bureau of Criminal Statistics and Special Services. 1995. *Crime and Delinquency in California, 1994.* Sacramento, California.

Camp, George M. and Camille Camp. 1997. *The Corrections Yearbook.* South Salem, New York: Criminal Justice Institute, Inc.

————. 1999. *The Corrections Yearbook.* Middletown, Connecticut: Criminal Justice Institute, Inc.

————. 2000. *The Corrections Yearbook.* Middletown, Connecticut: Criminal Justice Institute, Inc.

Cintron, Myrna and W. Wesley Johnson. 1996. "The Modern Plague: Controlling Substance Abuse." In Timothy J. Flanagan and Dennis R. Longmire, eds. *Americans View Crime and Justice: A National Public Opinion Survey.* Thousand Oaks, California: Sage Publications.125-136.

Clear, Todd. 1988. "Statistical Prediction in Corrections." *Research in Corrections.* Washington, D.C.: U.S. Department of Justice, National Institute of Corrections. 1:1-39.

————. 1994. *Harm in American Penology.* Albany, New York: State University of New York Press.

Clear, Todd and Anthony A. Braga. 1995. "Community Corrections." In James Q. Wilson and Joan Petersilia, eds. *Crime.* San Francisco, California: Institute for Contemporary Studies. 421- 444.

Clear, Todd R. and George C. Cole. 1997. *American Corrections*, 4th edition. Belmont, California: Wadsworth Publishing.

Comptroller General of the United States. 1976. *State and County Probation: Systems in Crisis, Report to the Congress of the United States.* Washington, D.C.: U.S. Government Printing Office.

Crouch, Ben. 1993. "Is Incarceration Really Worse? Analysis of Offenders' Preferences for Prisons over Probation." *Justice Quarterly.*10: 67-88.

Cunniff, Mark and Ilene R. Bergsmann. 1990. *Managing Felons in the Community: An Administrative Profile of Probation.* Washington, D.C.: The National Association of Criminal Justice Planners.

Cunniff, Mark and Mary Shilton. 1991. *Variations on Felony Probation: Persons under Supervision in 32 Urban and Suburban Counties.* Washington, D.C.: U.S. Department of Justice.

Dawson, John. 1990. *Felony Probation in State Courts.* Washington, D.C.: U.S. Department of Justice, Bureau of Justice Statistics.

del Carmen, Rolando V. and James Alan Pilant. 1994. "The Scope of Judicial Immunity for Probation and Parole Officers." *Perspectives.* 14-21.

Deschenes, Elizabeth, Susan Turner, and Peter Greenwood. 1995. "Drug Court or Probation: An Experimental Evaluation of Maricopa County's Drug Court." *Justice System Journal.* 18,1:55-73.

Dressler, David. 1962. *Practice and Theory of Probation and Parole.* New York: Columbia University Press.

Falco, Malthea. 1995. *Keeping Score: What Are We Getting for Our Federal Drug Control Dollars?* Washington, D.C.: Drug Strategies.

Finn, Peter and Dale Parent. 1992. *Making the Offender Foot the Bill: A Texas Program.* Washington, D.C.: U.S. Department of Justice, National Institute of Justice.

Fitzharris, Timothy L. 1979. *Probation in an Era of Diminishing Resources.* Sacramento, California: The Foundation for Continuing Education in Corrections: The California Probation, Parole, and Correctional Association.

Flanagan, Timothy J. and Dennis R. Longmire. 1996. *Americans View Crime and Justice: A National Public Opinion Survey*. Thousand Oaks, California: Sage Publications.

Frank, J., F. Cullen, and J. Cullen.1987. "Sources of Judicial Attitudes Toward Criminal Sanctioning." *American Journal of Crime and Justice*. 11.

Gebelein, Richard S. 2000. "The Rebirth of Rehabilitation: Promise and Perils of Drug Courts." Washington, D.C.: U.S. Department of Justice, National Institute of Justice.

Geerken, Michael and Hennessey D. Hayes. 1993. "Probation and Parole: Public Risk and the Future of Incarceration Alternatives." *Criminology*. 31, 4:549-564.

Gendreau, Paul. 1996. "The Principles of Effective Intervention with Offenders." In Alan Harland, ed. *Choosing Correctional Options that Work: Defining the Demand then Evaluating the Supply*. Thousand Oaks, California: Sage. 117-130.

Gerstein, Dean, R. A. Johnson, H. J. Harwood, D. Fountain, N. Suter, and K. Malloy. 1994. *Evaluating Recovery Services: The California Drug and Alcohol Treatment Assessment*. Sacramento, California: Department of Alcohol and Drug Programs, State of California.

Goldkamp, John. 1994. "Miami's Treatment Drug Court for Felony Misdemeanants." *The Prison Journal*. 73:110-166.

Gowdy, Voncile. 1993. *Intermediate Sanctions*. Washington, D.C.: U.S. Department of Justice, National Institute of Justice.

Gowen, Darren. 2000. "Overview of the Federal Home Confinement Program 1988-1996." *Federal Probation*. 64(2), 11-18.

Greenwood, Peter, C. Peter Rydell, Allan F. Abrahamse, Jonathan P. Caulkins, James Chiesa, Karyn E. Model, and Steve Klein. 1994. *Three Strikes and You're Out: Estimated Benefits and Costs of California's New Mandatory-Sentencing Law*. Santa Monica, California: RAND.

Griffin, Margaret. 1996. "Hunt County, Texas, Puts Performance-Based Measures to Work." *Perspectives*. American Probation and Parole Association. 9:11.

Grubbs, John. 1993. "Handling Probation and Parole Violators in Mississippi." In Edward Rhine, ed. *Reclaiming Offender Accountability: Intermediate Sanctions for Probation and Parole Violators*. Laurel, Maryland: American Correctional Association. 62-68.

Hamai, K., R. Ville, R. Harris, M. Hough, and Ugljesa Zvedkic, eds. 1995. *Probation Round the World*. London: Routledge.

Harland, Alan T. 1996. "Correctional Options That Work: Structuring the Inquiry." In Alan T. Harland, ed. *Choosing Correctional Options That Work: Defining the Demand and Evaluating the Supply*. Thousand Oaks, California: Sage Publications. 1-17.

Harris, M. Kay. 2001. *Trends and Issues in Community Corrections Acts*. Philadelphia: Crime and Justice Research Institute.

Harris, Philip and Stephen Smith. 1996. "Developing Community Corrections: An Implementation Perspective." In Alan Harland, ed. *Choosing Correctional Options That Work: Defining the Demand and Evaluating the Supply*. Thousand Oaks, California: Sage Publications. 183-222.

Hart, Timothy C. and Brian A. Reaves. 1999. *Felony Defendants in Large Urban Counties 1996*. Washington, D.C.: U.S. Department of Justice, Bureau of Justice Statistics.

Herman, Paul D. 1993. "Missouri's Response to Technical Violators." In Edward E. Rhine, ed. *Intermediate Sanctions for Probation and Parole Violators*. Laurel, Maryland: American Correctional Association.

Howell, James C., Barry Krisberg, and Michael Jones. 1993. "Trends in Juvenile Crime and Youth Violence." In James C. Howell et al., eds. *Serious, Violent and Chronic Juvenile Offenders: A Sourcebook*. Thousand Oaks, California: Sage Publications.

Hurst, H. and Patricia Torbet. 1993. *Organization and Administration of Juvenile Services: Probation, Aftercare, and State Institutions for Delinquent Youth*. Washington, D.C.: U.S. Department of Justice, Office of Juvenile Justice and Delinquency Prevention.

Institute of Medicine. 1990. Committee for the Substance Abuse Coverage Study (D. R. Gerstein and H. J. Harwood, eds.), *Treating Drug Problems, Vol. 1, A Study of the Evolution, Effectiveness, and Financing of Public and Private Drug Treatment Systems*. Washington D.C.: National Academy Press.

Jones, Peter R. 1996. "Risk Prediction in Criminal Justice." In Alan T. Harland, ed. *Choosing Correctional Options That Work: Defining the Demand and Evaluating the Supply*. Thousand Oaks, California: Sage Publications. 33-68.

Klein, Andrew R. 1997. *Alternative Sentencing, Intermediate Sanctions, and Probation*. Cincinnati, Ohio: Anderson Publishing Company.

Klein, Stephen, Patricia Ebener, Allan Abrahamse, Nora Fitzgerald. 1991. *Predicting Criminal Justice Outcomes: What Matters?* Santa Monica, California: RAND.

Langan, Patrick. 1994. "Between Prison and Probation: Intermediate Sanctions." *Science*. 264:791-93.

————. 1996. Personal communication. Washington D.C.: U.S. Department of Justice, Bureau of Justice Statistics.

Langan, Patrick and Mark A. Cunniff. 1992. *Recidivism of Felons on Probation, 1986-89.* Washington D.C.: U.S. Department of Justice, Bureau of Justice Statistics.

Langan, Patrick and Helen Graziadei. 1995. *Felony Sentencing in State Courts, 1992.* Washington, D.C.: U.S. Department of Justice, Bureau of Justice Statistics.

Latessa, Edward J., ed. 1999. *Strategic Solutions: The International Community Corrections Association Examines Substance Abuse.* Lanham, Maryland: International Community Corrections Association and American Correctional Association.

Latessa, Edward J. and Harry E. Allen. 1997. *Corrections in the Community.* Cincinnati, Ohio: Anderson Publishing Company.

Lehman, Joseph D. 2001. "Re-Inventing Community Corrections in Washington State." *Corrections Management Quarterly.* 5.

Levin, David J., Patrick A. Langan, and Jodi M. Brown. 2000. *State Court Sentencing of Convicted Felons, 1996.* Washington D.C.: U.S. Department of Justice, Bureau of Justice Statistics.

Linden, Russ. 1996. "Making Improvements by Hook or by Crook: Reengineering New York City's Probation Department." New York: Reengineering Resource Center.

Lipton, Douglas S. 1995. *The Effectiveness of Treatment for Drug Abusers Under Criminal Justice Supervision.* Washington D.C.: U.S. Department of Justice, National Institute of Justice.

Los Angeles County Planning Committee. 1996. *Managing Offenders in Los Angeles County.* Los Angeles, California.

Los Angeles County Probation Department. 2001. Available http://probation.co.la.ca.us/.

Lyons, Donna H. 2001. "Criminal Justice: State Crime Legislation in 2000." *State Legislative Report.* 26(1). Denver, Colorado: National Conference of State Legislatures.

Maquire, Kathleen and Ann L. Pastore, eds. 1995. *Sourcebook of Criminal Justice Statistics 1994.* Washington, D.C.: U.S. Department of Justice, Bureau of Justice Statistics.

Martinson, Robert. 1974. "What Works? Questions and Answers about Prison Reform." *The Public Interest.* 35:22-54.

Mauer, Marc and Tracy Huling. 1995. *Young Black Americans and the Criminal Justice System: Five Years Later.* Washington, D.C.: The Sentencing Project.

McAnany, Patrick, Doug Thomson, and David Fogel. 1984. *Probation and Justice: Reconsideration of Mission.* Cambridge, Massachusetts: Oelgeschlager, Gunn and Hain.

McDonald, D. C. and K. E. Carlson. 1993. *Sentencing in the Federal Courts: Does Race Matter?* Washington, D.C.: U.S. Department of Justice, Bureau of Justice Statistics.

McShane, Marilyn and Wesley Krause. 1993. *Community Corrections.* New York: Macmillan Publishing Company.

Minnesota Sentencing Guidelines Commission. 1996. *Sentencing Practices: Highlights and Statistics Tables.* St. Paul, Minnesota: Minnesota Sentencing Guidelines Commission.

Morgan, Kathryn. 1993. "Factors Influencing Probation Outcome: A Review of the Literature." *Federal Probation.* 57(2):23-29.

Morgan, Terry and Stephen Marris. 1994. "Washington's Partnership Between the Police and Community Corrections: A Program Worth Emulating." *Perspectives.* 28-30.

Morris, Norval, and Michael Tonry. 1990. *Between Probation and Punishment: Intermediate Punishments in a Rational Sentencing System.* New York: Oxford.

Mulholland, David. 1994. "Judges Finding Creative Ways of Punishing." *Wall Street Journal.* May 24. B:1.

National Advisory Commission on Criminal Justice Standards and Goals. 1973. *Corrections.* Washington D.C.: U.S. Government Printing Office.

National Institute of Corrections. 1993. *State and Local Probation Systems in the United States: A Survey of Current Practice.* Washington, D.C.: U.S. Department of Justice.

————. 1999. *State Organizational Structures for Delivering Adult Probation Services.* Washington, D.C.: U.S. Department of Justice.

Nelson, E. Kim, Howard Ohmart, and Nora Harlow. 1978. *Promising Strategies in Probation and Parole.* Washington, D.C: U.S. Government Printing Office.

Nidorf, Barry. 1996. "Surviving in a 'Lock Them Up' Era." *Federal Probation.* 60: 1.

Office of Justice Programs. 1998. *Rethinking Probation: Community Supervision, Community Safety.* Washington, D.C.: U.S. Department of Justice, Office of Justice Programs.

Office of National Drug Control Policy. 1996. *The National Drug Control Strategy, 1996.* Washington D.C.: Office of National Drug Control Policy.

O'Leary, Vincent and Todd R. Clear. 1984. *Directions for Community Corrections in the 1990s.* Washington, D.C.: U.S. Department of Justice, National Institute of Corrections.

Parent, Dale G. 1995. "Community Corrections Acts: A Recap." *Overcrowded Times*. 6, 5:1, 9-11.

Parent, Dale, Dan Wentwork, Peggy Burke, and Becky Ney. 1994. *Responding to Probation and Parole Violations*. Washington D.C.: U.S. Department of Justice, National Institute of Justice.

Parent, Dale, et al. 1995. *Day Reporting Centers*. Washington, D. C.: U.S. Department of Justice, National Institute of Justice.

Parent, Dale, et al. 1997. "Key Legislative Issues in Criminal Justice: Intermediate Sanctions." Washington, D. C.: U.S. Department of Justice, National Institute of Justice.

Perkins, Craig. 1994. *National Corrections Reporting Program, 1992*. Washington, D.C.: U.S. Department of Justice, Bureau of Justice Statistics.

Peter D. Hart Associates, Inc.1994. "American Attitudes Toward the Drug Problem and Drug Policy." Study #3942. Washington, D.C.: Peter D. Hart Associates, Inc.

Petersilia, Joan. 1992. "California's Prison Policy: Causes, Costs, and Consequences." *The Prison Journal*. 72: 1.

———. 1993. "Measuring the Performance of Community Corrections." In *Performance Measures for the Criminal Justice System*. Washington, D.C.: U.S. Department of Justice, Bureau of Justice Statistics. 61-87.

———. 1995a. "How California Could Divert Nonviolent Prisoners to Intermediate Sanctions." *Overcrowded Times*. 4-8.

———. 1995b. "A Crime Control Rationale for Reinvesting in Community Corrections." *The Prison Journal*. 75: 4.

———. 1998. "A Decade of Experimenting with Intermediate Sanctions: What Have We Learned?" In *Perspectives on Crime and Justice: 1997-1998 Lecture Series, Vol. 2, Research Forum*. Washington, D.C.: U.S. Department of Justice, National Institute of Justice.

———. 2000. "When Prisoners Return to the Community: Political, Economic, and Social Consequences." Washington, D.C.: U.S. Department of Justice, National Institute of Justice.

Petersilia, Joan and Elizabeth Piper Deschenes. 1994. "Perceptions of Punishment: Inmates and Staff Rank the Severity of Prison versus Intermediate Sanctions." *The Prison Journal*. 74: 306-328.

Petersilia, Joan and Susan Turner. 1986. *Prison Versus Probation in California: Implications for Crime and Offender Recidivism.* Santa Monica, California: RAND.

―――. 1993. "Intensive Probation and Parole." In Michael Tonry, ed. *Crime and Justice: An Annual Review of Research.* Chicago: University of Chicago Press. 281-335.

Petersilia, Joan, Susan Turner, James Kahan, and Joyce Peterson. 1985. *Granting Felons Probation: Public Risks and Alternatives.* Santa Monica, California: RAND.

Prendergast, Michael, Douglas Anglin, and Jean Wellisch. 1995. "Treatment for Drug-Abusing Offenders Under Community Supervision." *Federal Probation.* 59, 4.

President's Commission on Law Enforcement and Administration of Justice. 1972. *The Challenge of Crime in a Free Society.* New York: Avon.

Prevost, John P., Edward Rhine, and Ronald Jackson, "The Parole Violations Process in Georgia." In Edward Rhine, ed. *Reclaiming Offender Accountability: Intermediate Sanctions for Probation and Parole Violators.* Lanham, Maryland: American Correctional Association. 52-61.

Puzzanchera, Charles, et al. 2000. *Juvenile Court Statistics 1997.* Washington, D.C.: U.S. Department of Justice, Office of Juvenile Justice and Delinquency Prevention.

Reaves, Brian A. and Pheny Z. Smith. 1995. *Felony Defendants in Large Urban Counties, 1992.* Washington, D.C.: U.S. Department of Justice, Bureau of Justice Statistics.

Reinventing Probation Council. 1999. "'Broken Windows' Probation: The Next Step in Fighting Crime." *Civic Report.* 7:2.

Rhine, Edward, ed. 1993. *Reclaiming Offender Accountability: Intermediate Sanctions for Probation and Parole Violators.* Lanham, Maryland: American Correctional Association.

Rosecrace, John. 1988. "Maintaining the Myth of Individualized Justice: Probation Persistence Reports." *Justice Quarterly.* 5:235-256.

Rothman, David J. 1980. *Conscience and Convenience: The Asylum and Its Alternatives in Progressive America.* Boston, Massachusetts: Little, Brown.

Shilton, Mary K. 1995. "Community Corrections Acts May be Rx Systems Need." *Corrections Today.* 57(1): 32-36, 66.

Siegh, E. 1993. "From Augustus to the Progressives: A Study of Probation's Formative Years." *Federal Probation.* 57(3):67-72.

Sigler, Robert and David Lamb. 1994. "Community Based Alternatives to Prison: How the Public and Court Personnel View Them." *Federal Probation.* 59, 2:3-9.

Skolnick, Jerome. 1990. "Gangs and Crime Old at Time, But Drugs Change Gang Culture." *Crime and Delinquency in California, 1989.* Sacramento, California: California Department of Corrections.

Smith, Michael, and Walter Dickey. 1998. "What if Corrections Were Serious about Public Safety?" *Corrections Management Quarterly.* 2: 12-30.

Solari, Richard. 1992. *National Judicial Report Program, 1988.* Washington, D.C.: U.S. Department of Justice, Bureau of Justice Statistics.

Spelman, William. 1995. "The Severity of Intermediate Sanctions." *Journal of Research in Crime and Delinquency.* 32:107-135.

Taxman, Faye S. 1995. "Intermediate Sanctions: Dealing with Technical Violators." *Corrections Today.* 57(1):46-57.

Taxman, Faye S. and James Byrne. 1994. "Locating Absconders: Results from a Randomized Field Experiment." *Federal Probation.* 58(1):13-23.

Taylor, Stan. 2000. "Violation of Probation Centers and the 'Broken Windows' Theory." In Lehman, Joseph. "Correctional Best Practices: Directors' Perspectives." *Association of State Correctional Administrators Newsletter.* August 2000. 183-185.

Thomas, Douglas. 1993. *The State of Juvenile Probation 1992: Results of a Nationwide Survey.* Washington, D.C.: U.S. Department of Justice, Office of Juvenile Justice and Delinquency Prevention.

Tonry, Michael and Mary Lynch. 1996. "Intermediate Sanctions." In *Crime and Justice: A Review of Research.* Chicago: University of Chicago Press. 99-144.

Torbet, Patricia McFall. 1996. *Juvenile Probation: The Workhorse of the Juvenile Justice System.* Washington, D.C.: U.S. Department of Justice, Office of Juvenile Justice and Delinquency Prevention.

Turner, Susan, Joan Petersilia, and Elizabeth Deschenes. 1994. "The Implementation and Effectiveness of Drug Testing in Community Supervision: Results of an Experimental Evaluation." In Doris L. McKenzie and Craig D. Uchida, eds. *Drugs and Crime: Evaluating Pubic Policy Initiatives.* Thousand Oaks, California: Sage Publications.

Vito, Gennaro F. 1985. "Probation as Punishment." In Lawrence F. Travis, ed. *Probation, Parole and Community Corrections: A Reader.* Prospect Heights, Illinois: Waveland Press, Inc. 73-80.

————. 1992. "Felony Probation and Recidivism: Replication and Response." In Lawrence F. Travis et al., eds. *Corrections: An Issues Approach.* Cincinnati, Ohio: Anderson.

Wilkinson, Reginald. 1995. *Community Corrections: A Vital Link*. Columbus: Ohio Department of Corrections.

Wilson, James Q. 1995. "Crime and Public Policy." In James Q. Wilson and Joan Petersilia, eds. *Crime*. San Francisco, California: Institute for Contemporary Studies. 489-510.

Wood, Peter B. and Harold G. Grasmick. 1995. "Inmates Rank the Severity of Ten Alternative Sanctions Compared to Prison." *Journal of the Oklahoma Criminal Justice Research Consortium*. 2:30-42.

Zvekic, Ugljesa. 1996. "Probation in International Perspective." *Overcrowded Times*. 7(2):5-8.

PART TWO

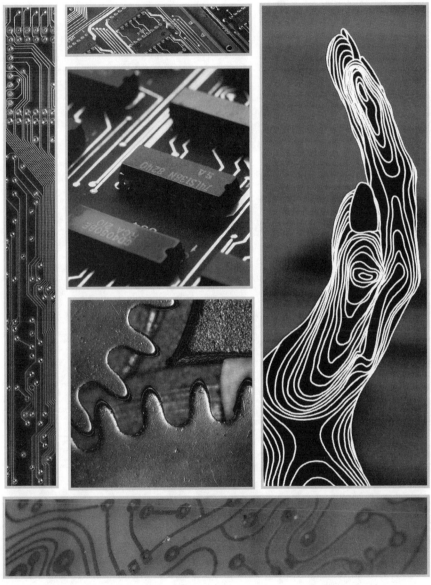

PAROLE AND PRISONER REENTRY
IN THE UNITED STATES

CHAPTER ONE

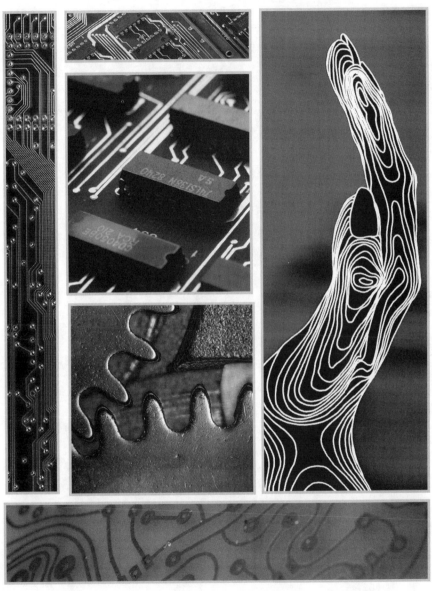

Parole and Prisoner Reentry in the
United States: An Introduction

Parole and Prisoner Reentry in the United States: An Introduction[1]

Public anger and frustration over crime continue to produce significant changes in the American criminal justice system, but reforms focused on parole are among the most profound. Parole, which is both a procedure by which a board administratively releases inmates from prison and a provision for post release supervision, has come to symbolize the leniency of the system, where inmates are "let out" early. When a parolee commits a particularly heinous crime, such as the kidnapping and murder of thirteen-year-old Polly Klaas by California parolee Richard Allen Davis, or the horrifying rape and murder of four-year-old Megan Kanka in New Jersey by a paroled sex offender, the public understandably is outraged and calls for "abolishing parole."

Parole Release Abolished

State legislatures have responded. And by the end of 2000, fourteen states had abolished early release by a parole board for all offenders. California still allows discretionary release by a parole board, but only for offenders with indeterminate life sentences (for example, first-degree murder or kidnapping for ransom) (Hughes, Wilson, and Beck, 2001). Even in states that have retained parole, parole boards have become more hesitant to grant it. In Texas, for example, 57

---

[1] This section has been updated and revised from "Parole and Prisoner Reentry in the United States" by Joan Petersilia, originally published by the University of Chicago in *Crime and Justice: A Review of Research*, Volume 26, 1999.

The author wishes to thank Allen Beck, Corrections Statistics Program, Bureau of Justice Statistics, U.S. Department of Justice, for his generous assistance in identifying and interpreting relevant parole data. Edward Rhine, Michael Tonry, Peggy Burke, Frances Cullen, and Gail Hughes also made helpful comments.

percent of all cases considered for parole release in 1988 were approved; but by 1998, that figure had dropped to just 20 percent (Fabelo, 1999). The state of New Jersey retains a "No Early Release Act" that forces violent criminals to serve 85 percent of their sentence before parole; twenty-nine states and Washington, D.C. enforce similar truth-in-sentencing laws (Hughes, Wilson, and Beck, 2001).

The argument for abolishing parole is that it will lead to longer prison sentences and greater honesty in sentencing decisions. George Allen, former Governor of Virginia, made abolishing parole a major campaign issue. Once elected governor in 1994, Allen eliminated that state's discretionary parole system for violent offenders. He proclaimed:

> The principle that has guided our efforts is honesty. Easy-release rules prevented judges and juries from pre-empting the community's judgement about proper punishment for illegal conduct. Under the new law, judges do not have to play guessing games when imposing sentences. Police officers do not have to see the criminals out on the streets only a year after their last arrest. Criminals know they cannot beat the system. Crime victims and their families finally are seeing justice done (Allen, 1997: 22).

Parole Release Weakened

But correctional experts argue that while abolishing parole may make good politics, it contributes to bad correctional practices—and ultimately, less public safety. As Burke (1995:11) notes, parole makes release from prison a privilege that must be earned. When states abolish parole or reduce the amount of discretion parole authorities have, they, in essence, replace a rational, controlled system of "earned" release for selected inmates, with "automatic" release for nearly all inmates. Proponents argue that the public does not understand the tremendous power that is lost when parole is abandoned. Through the exercise of its discretion, parole boards actually can target more violent and dangerous offenders for longer periods of incarceration. Burke (1995:11) writes:

> The absence of parole means that offenders simply walk out of the door of prison at the end of a pre-determined period of time, no questions asked. No human being

asks the tough questions about what has been done to make sure this criminal is no longer a danger before he is released.

In fact, the case of Richard Allen Davis is a perfect example. The California Board of Prison Terms (the parole board) knew the risks he posed, and had denied him parole in each of the six instances where his case had been reviewed. But once California abolished discretionary parole release, the Board of Prison Terms no longer had the authority to deny release to inmates whose new standard sentence mandated automatic release after serving a set portion of their terms. Release dates were calculated by the computer for thousands of prisoners then in custody, and when it was determined that Mr. Davis already had served the amount of prison time that the new law required, he had to be released. Less than four months later, he murdered Polly Klaas. California parole officials suspect that had the state not abolished parole, Mr. Davis would never have been released (Burke, 1995). Similarly, the case of the murderer of Megan Kanka was never heard by a parole board; rather, he went out of prison under mandatory release.

Eliminating parole boards also means that several important ancillary purposes of parole also are eliminated. Parole boards have the ability to "individualize sentencing," and as such can provide a review mechanism for assuring greater uniformity in sentencing across judges or counties. Parole boards also can take into account changes in the offender's behavior that might have occurred after he or she was incarcerated. Imprisonment can cause psychological breakdowns, depression, or mental illnesses, and the parole board can adjust release dates to account for these changes. Finally, abolishing parole boards also eliminates the major mechanism by which crowded prisons can quickly reduce populations. The Urban Institute notes that, because of sentencing reform (which has accompanied parole reduction), released prisoners on average are serving longer sentences (Travis, Solomon, and Waul, 2001).

As parole expert Vincent O'Leary once observed: "Most people start out reforming parole, but when you pull that string you find a lot more attached" (Wilson, 1977: 49). Crowded prisons illustrate this clearly. Reforming parole release practices requires additional attention to the supervisory roles parole plays.

Parole Supervision Failures Reconsidered

Until recently, the lines were drawn between tough-on-crime "abolitionists" and parole-as-rehabilitation "traditionalists." Politicians continued to shout "abolish parole," while corrections professionals asked for more money to invest in services and surveillance, and the two seemed worlds apart. Recently, however, politicians seem to be listening more closely to the professionals, as parole—or more precisely, failure on parole—is creating severe fiscal pressures on state prisons' budgets. A greater number of parolees are failing supervision and being returned to prison, and as a result, contributing disproportionately to prison crowding and the continued pressure to build more prisons. As New York Assemblyman Daniel L. Feldman warned: "Lock 'em up and throw away the key attitudes are coming back to haunt state legislators across the nation" (Carter, 1998: 2). An excellent case study is parole revocations in California.

In California, 117,000 adults are now on parole (one out of every six U.S. parolees), and nearly 75 percent are failing to successfully complete supervision (Hughes, Wilson, and Beck, 2001). It is debatable to what degree parole violators contribute to California's staggering recidivism rate (57.8 percent in 1999) (Camp and Camp, 2000). Parole violators accounted for 67 percent of all California prison admissions in 1997, and 41 percent of prison admissions were for violations of the technical conditions of parole, rather than for the conviction of new crimes (Hughes, Wilson, and Beck, 2001; Austin and Lawson, 1998). It should be noted, however, that a technical violation does not mean the inmate was not engaged in criminal behavior. It may be that the inmate was arrested for a criminal charge but in lieu of prosecution, was revoked and returned to custody. In fact, the vast majority of these technical violations (82 percent) have an underlying criminal charge (Austin and Lawson, 1998).

When revoked to prison, California inmates spend an additional three to four months in prison prior to being re-released (Little Hoover Commission, 1998). Recent analyses suggest that such "high parole revocation rates presents an enormous waste of prison resources and does not fit the mission of a traditional state prison system (in other words, the long-term confinement of sentenced felons)"

(Austin and Lawson, 1998:13). One response to the kinds of problems California faces is to propose abolishing both parole release and supervision.

Parole Supervision Restored and Renamed

A few states not only have abolished parole release, but also have considered abolishing parole supervision (often referred to as the "other" parole). In Maine, the legislature not only abolished the parole board but also abolished parole supervision. Similarly, when Virginia abolished parole release, they also abolished parole supervision. Unless the judge remembers to impose a split sentence with a term of probation to follow prison, offenders leave Virginia prisons with no strings attached. When states abolish parole supervision along with parole release, they lose the ability to supervise or provide services to released inmates when they have the highest risk of recidivism and are most in need of services.

Several states that at one point abolished discretionary parole release have reestablished its equivalent. North Carolina, which placed severe constraints on its parole commission in 1981, gradually has restored some of its previous discretion. Florida, which adopted sentencing guidelines in 1983 and abolished parole, now has returned the function under the new name, *Controlled Release Authority*. Colorado abolished discretionary parole release in 1979 and reinstated it six years later. Elected officials, along with law enforcement and corrections professionals, lobbied to reinstate parole release and supervision after data suggested that the length of prison sentence served actually had decreased following the elimination of parole, and the ability to provide surveillance or treatment of high-risk offenders had declined significantly. As Bill Woodward, then-director of the Division of Criminal Justice in Colorado, noted: "[T]he problem with abolishing parole is you lose your ability to keep track of the inmates and the ability to keep them in treatment if they have alcohol and drug problems" (Gainsborough, 1997:12).

Today, all states except Maine and Virginia have some requirement for post-prison or parole supervision, and nearly 80 percent of all released prisoners in 1999 were subject to some form of conditional community or supervised release (Ditton and Wilson, 1999; Hughes, Wilson, and Beck, 2001). However, some states have changed its name to distance themselves from the negative connotation that "parole" has. For example, postprison supervision is called *community control* in Ohio, *supervised release* in Minnesota and in the federal system, and *community custody* in Washington. Parole services are overseen in Arizona by the *Board of Executive Clemency* and provided in Arkansas by the *Department of Community Punishment*. Regardless of its name, however, parole supervision has changed significantly during the past decade, as national support for parole-as-rehabilitation has waned (Petersilia, 2000).

Parole Services Depleted

Parole officers readily admit they have fewer services to offer an ever-growing population of offenders. Safety and security have become major issues in parole services (Lynch, 1998), and parole officers now are authorized to carry weapons in two-thirds of the states (Camp and Camp, 1999). One recent study of prisoner reentry cites survey results that show most parole officers give higher priority to law enforcement services than to rehabilitative services (Travis, Solomon, and Waul, 2001). Parole officers in most large urban areas are now more surveillance- than services-oriented, and drug testing, electronic monitoring and verifying curfews are the most common activities of many parole agents (Petersilia, 1998b).

Parole was founded primarily to foster offender reformation rather than to increase punitiveness or surveillance. Abandoning parole's historical commitment to rehabilitation worries correctional professionals. The reality is that more than nine out of ten prisoners are released back into the community, and with an average (median) U.S. prison term served of fifteen months, half of all inmates in U.S. prisons today will be back on the streets in less than two years (Beck, 1999). Overall, almost 40 percent of annual admissions to state prisons are repeat court commitments, including parole violators (a 10 percent increase over the past decade) (Beck, 2000). The transition from prison back into the community is exceedingly difficult, and recidivism rates are highest in the first year following release. A study by the Bureau of Justice Statistics found that 25 percent of released prisoners are rearrested in the first six months, and 40 percent within the first year (Beck and Shipley, 1989).

To assist in this high-risk time period, parole historically has provided job assistance, family counseling, and chemical dependency programs (although, arguably, never enough of them). According to a recent survey, most parole systems offer outgoing inmates vocational training, education, and job seeking skills programs. However, fewer than half reported providing substance abuse treatment, anger management classes, life skills programs, or family parenting help as pre- or postrelease services (American Correctional Association, 2001a). And a recent Urban Institute study notes that, between 1991 and 1997, there was a decrease in participation in prerelease, educational, and vocational programs (Travis, Solomon, and Waul, 2001). Punitive public attitudes, combined with diminishing social service resources, have resulted in fewer services provided to parolees.

What Works?

Parole, a system that developed in the United States more by accident than by design, now threatens to become the tail that wagged corrections' dog. Prison populations continue to rise, more offenders are required to be on parole supervision, where fewer services and work programs exist due to scarcity of resources (often diverted from parole services to fund prison expansion). A greater number of parole violations (particularly drug use) are detected through monitoring and drug testing, and parole authorities have increasingly less tolerance for failure. Revocation to prison is becoming a predictable (and increasingly short) transition in the prison-to-parole and back-to-prison revolving door cycle. Correctional leaders and many elected officials acknowledge parole does not work, and increasingly are asking, "Must they all come back?"

Of course, answering that question is exceedingly complex. We would need to know what kinds of programs reduce recidivism for offenders with different needs. Would more intensive surveillance lower recidivism, and how intense must it be to make a difference? What combination of conditions, surveillance, and treatment gets the best results? Once we have identified programs that make a difference, we would have to ask a number of additional questions. For example, should we mandate that parolees participate in needed treatment, or simply make it available to those who volunteer? How long should parole last? Should some parolees be kept on "banked" caseloads, with no services or supervision, simply to expedite their return to prison if they commit new crimes? What difference does caseload size make, and which kinds of officers are more successful with which kinds of clients? These are tough questions, and sound bite attacks on parole are not very helpful in answering them.

Reinventing Rehabilitative Parole

While the public is not lenient about crime, there is some data that suggests they do believe in parole and rehabilitation. The American public of the 1970s, reacting to the failure of individualized treatment to rehabilitate violent offenders, began to look more favorably upon longer sentences and greater difficulty for offenders desiring parole (Fagan, 1998). However, by 1985, the Figgie Report found that only 8 percent of the pubic polled called for parole to be eliminated entirely. Almost a quarter of those polled thought parole should remain intact, and over half hoped it would be retained but reorganized (Freeman, 2000). Further, the American Correctional Association, analyzing a recent survey of parole systems, concludes: "It appears that the unfavorable reputation parole experienced in the early 1990s, which caused several jurisdictions to terminate it, has changed. . . . [T]here is little desire to further eliminate parole" (American Correctional Association, 2001a).

We need to begin a serious dialog aimed at "reinventing" parole in the United States so that it better balances the public's need to hold offenders accountable with the need to provide services to released offenders. To begin that dialog, we first need to assemble information on what is known about parole in the United States.

Organization of "Parole and Prisoner Reentry in the United States"

Chapter 2 begins by describing sources of U.S. adult parole data; juvenile data or practices are not considered. Chapter 3 discusses the early evolution of parole in the United States and its use in modern sentencing practices. This section reviews the dramatic changes in parole release that resulted from the nation's skepticism about the ability of prisons to rehabilitate.

Chapter 4 describes the current parole population. It presents trend data on the growth of the parole population, and what is known about parolees' crimes, personal backgrounds, and court-ordered conditions. It also presents data on the

H

average size of parole caseloads, offender contact requirements, and annual costs of supervision. Chapter 5 is devoted to describing offenders' needs as they transition to the community, and describes what services are available to meet these needs. This section also outlines the civil disabilities that apply to ex-convicts.

Chapter 6 assesses parole outcomes and reviews parole completion and recidivism rates. Chapter 7 discusses some current thinking on how to reform parole, and identifies some of the more promising parole programs. Chapter 8 presents concluding remarks.

CHAPTER TWO

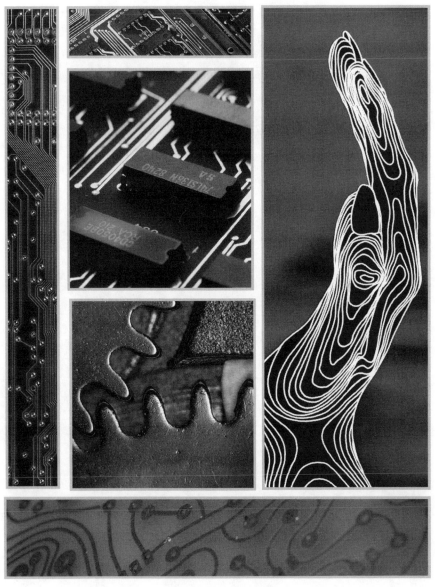

Sources of Parole Information

Federal Sources of Data

Various agencies within the U.S. Department of Justice collect most of the available information regarding current parole practices and parolee characteristics. Since 1990, the National Institute of Corrections (NIC) has supported periodic surveys that describe parole board practices in the United States (Rhine et al., 1991) and current state discretionary parole release practices (National Institute of Corrections, 1995). The Bureau of Justice Assistance (BJA) also has published a survey of state sentencing and parole practices (Austin et al., 1996).

Most of what we know about U.S. parolee characteristics comes from the Bureau of Justice Statistics (BJS), the statistical arm of the U.S. Department of Justice. Since the early 1980s, the Bureau of Justice Statistics has reported on the number of persons entering and exiting parole through its "National Corrections Reporting Program." This series collects data nearly every year on all prison admissions and releases and on all parole entries and discharges in participating jurisdictions.

The Bureau of Justice Statistics' "National Probation and Parole Reporting Program" gathers annual data on state and federal probation and parole counts and movements and the characteristics of persons under the supervision of probation and parole agencies. Published data include admissions and releases by method of entry and discharge. The Bureau of Justice Statistics also sponsors censuses, usually conducted every five to six years, describing the agencies that have control of persons serving a criminal sentence. The "Census of State and Local Probation and Parole Agencies," first conducted in 1991, gathers data on the agency organizational location, staffing, expenditures, and programs. Additionally, the Bureau of Justice Statistics issued a Special Report on "Trends in State Parole, 1990-2000" in October, 2001. Finally, the Bureau of Justice Statistics conducts surveys of jail and prison inmates (usually done every five years) that ask offenders whether they were on parole at the time of the arrest that led to their current conviction.

Other Sources of Data

Also conducting periodic studies are the nation's major parole associations: the American Probation and Parole Association (APPA); the American Correctional Association (ACA); and the Association of Paroling Authorities, International (APAI), which have conducted periodic studies (Burke, 1995; Rhine et al., 1991; and Runda et al., 1994).

Parole was not always such a minimal topic of data collection and research. Between 1965 and 1977, the National Council on Crime and Delinquency (NCCD) directed the "Uniform Parole Reports" project, which collected arrest, conviction, and imprisonment data on parolees. Analyses of this data helped researchers to improve methods for predicting parolee behavior (Gottfredson, Hoffman, and Sigler, 1975). The National Council on Crime and Delinquency data collection effort was discontinued in 1977, and no similar effort replaced it.

At about the same time, the U.S. Board of Parole undertook a major research study to develop parole guidelines, which incorporated offense seriousness and risk of recidivism (Gottfredson, Wilkins, and Hoffman, 1978). This research tracked released federal prisoners, and used the recidivism data to create an actuarial device, which in turn, was applied to each inmate to create a "Salient Factor Score" (SFS). The salient factor score provided explicit guidelines for release decisions based on a determination of the potential risk of parole violation (Hoffman and DeGostin, 1974). The Salient Factor Score was adopted by the U.S. Parole Board in 1972 and remained in use until the abolition of parole at the federal level in 1997.

Further Data Collection Needed

Beyond these early studies and the minimal descriptive data that is now collected, scant attention has been paid parole by the research or scholarly community.

We have very few parole program evaluations, or research studies of the parole process and its impact on offenders. The National Institute of Justice (NIJ), the research arm of the U.S. Department of Justice, has funded most of what has been conducted, which includes evaluations of drug testing for high risk parolees in Texas (Turner and Petersilia, 1992); intensive parole supervision in Minnesota (Deschenes, Turner, and Petersilia, 1995); work release in Washington (Turner and Petersilia, 1996a); and the effects of providing work training and day programs to parolees (Finn, 1998a; 1998b; and 1998c).

Parole has never attracted much scholarly interest, although a few notable exceptions include von Hirsch and Hanrahan,1979; Bottomly, 1990; Rhine, et al. 1991; McCleary, 1992; Simon, 1993; Richards, 1995; Abadinsky, 1997; Lynch, 1998; Cromwell and del Carmen, 1999; and Travis, Solomon, and Waul, 2001.

CHAPTER THREE

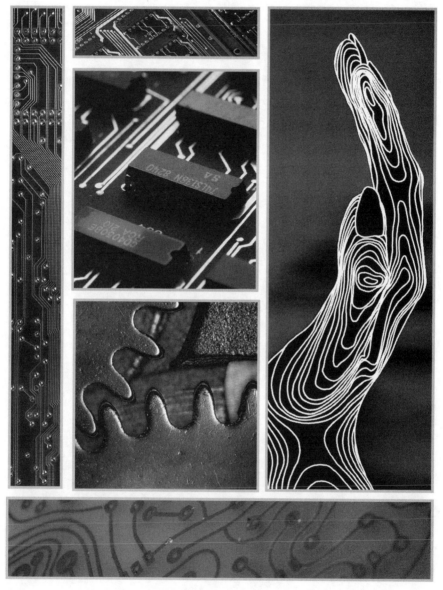

The Origins and Evolution of Parole in the United States

Early European Foundations and Growth of Parole

Parole comes from the French *parol*, referring to "word," as in giving one's word of honor or promise. It has come to mean an inmate's promise to conduct himself or herself in a law-abiding manner and according to certain rules in exchange for release. Parole is part of the general nineteenth-century trend in criminology that progressed from punishment to reformation.

Chief credit for developing the early parole system usually is given to Alexander Maconochie (1787-1860), who was in charge of the English penal colony at Norfolk Island, 1,000 miles off the coast of Australia, and to Sir Walter Crofton (1815-1897), who directed Ireland's prisons (Cromwell and del Carmen, 1999).

Maconochie criticized definite prison terms and developed a system of rewards for good conduct, labor, and study. Through a classification procedure he called *the mark system*, prisoners could progress through stages of increasing responsibility and ultimately gain freedom. In 1840, he was given an opportunity to apply these principles as superintendent of the Norfolk Island penal settlement in the South Pacific. Under his direction, task accomplishment, not time served, was the criterion for release. Marks of commendation were given to prisoners who performed their tasks well, and they were released from the penal colony as they demonstrated a willingness to accept society's rules.

Returning to England in 1844 to campaign for penal reform, Maconochie tried to implement his reforms when he was appointed governor of the new Birmingham Borough Prison in 1849. However, he was unable to institute his reforms there because he was dismissed from his position in 1851 on the grounds that his methods were too lenient (Clear and Cole, 1997).

Walter Crofton attempted to implement Maconochie's mark system when he became the administrator of the Irish Prison System in 1854. Crofton felt that prison programs should be directed more toward reformation, and that "tickets-of-leave" should be awarded to prisoners who had shown definitive achievement and positive attitude change. After instituting strict imprisonment, Crofton began transferring offenders to "intermediate prisons" where they could accumulate marks based on work performance, behavior, and educational improvement. Eventually, they would be given tickets-of-leave and released on parole supervision. Parolees were required to submit monthly reports to the police, and a police inspector helped them find jobs and generally oversaw their activities. The concepts of intermediate prisons, assistance, and supervision after release were Crofton's contributions to the modern system of parole (Clear and Cole, 1997).

The Genesis of American Parole

By 1865, American penal reformers were well aware of the reforms achieved in the European prison systems, particularly in the Irish system. At the Cincinnati meeting of the National Prison Association in 1870, a paper by Crofton was read, and specific references to the Irish system were incorporated into the "Declaration of Principles," along with other such reforms as indeterminate sentencing and classification for release based on a mark system. Because of Crofton's experiment, many Americans referred to parole as "the Irish system" (Walker, 1998).

Zebulon Brockway (1827-1920), a Michigan penologist, is given credit for implementing the first parole system in the United States. He proposed a two-pronged strategy for managing prison populations and preparing inmates for release: indeterminate sentencing coupled with parole supervision. He was given a chance to put his proposal into practice in 1876 when he was appointed superintendent at a new youth reformatory, the Elmira Reformatory in New York. He instituted a system of indeterminacy and parole release and is commonly credited as the father of both in the United States. His ideas reflected the tenor of the times—a belief that criminals could be reformed and that every prisoner's treatment should be individualized.

On being admitted to Elmira, each inmate (males between the ages of sixteen and thirty) was placed in the second grade of classification. Six months of good conduct meant promotion to the first grade—misbehavior could result in being placed in the third grade, from which the inmate would have to work his way back up. Continued good behavior in the first grade resulted in release. Paroled inmates remained under the jurisdiction of authorities for an additional six months, during which the parolee was required to report on the first day of every month to his appointed volunteer guardian (from which parole officers evolved) and provide an account of his situation and conduct (Abadinsky, 1997). Written reports became required and, after being signed by the parolee's employer and guardian, were submitted to the institute.

The Emergence of Modern Parole

Indeterminate sentencing and parole spread rapidly throughout the United States. In 1907, New York became the first state to formally adopt all the components of a parole system: indeterminate sentences, a system for granting release, postrelease supervision, and specific criteria for parole revocation. By 1927, only three states (Florida, Mississippi, and Virginia) were without a parole system, and by 1942, all states and the federal government had such systems (Clear and Cole, 1997).

The percentage of U.S. prisoners released on parole rose from 44 percent in 1940 to a high of 72 percent in 1977, after which some states began to question the very foundations of parole, and the number of prisoners released in this fashion began to decline (Bottomly, 1990). As shown in Figure 1, just 28 percent of prison releases were paroled in 1997. This is the lowest figure since the federal government began compiling statistics on this issue (Ditton and Wilson, 1999). Mandatory releases—the required release of inmates at the expiration of a certain time period—now surpass parole releases. And if one adds the "expiration releases," where the inmate is released after serving his or her full sentence, there is even a bigger imbalance between discretionary parole and mandatory release (28 percent versus 57 percent).

FIGURE 1: PERCENT OF STATE PRISONERS RELEASED BY VARIOUS METHODS

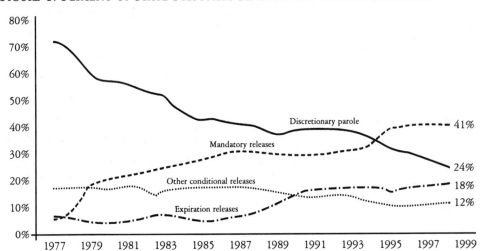

Note: *Discretionary parolees* are persons entering the community because of a parole board decision. *Mandatory releases* are persons whose release from prison was not decided by a parole board. This includes those entering because of determinate sentencing statutes, good-time provisions, or emergency releases. Other conditional releases include commutations, pardons, and deaths. Expiration releases are those where the inmate has served his or her maximum court sentence. Source: Bureau of Justice Statistics, National Prisoner Statistics, 1977-1997; Bureau of Justice Statistics, Trends in State Parole, 1990-2000.

Parole, it seemed during the first half of the twentieth century, made perfect sense. First, it was believed to contribute to prisoner reform by encouraging participation in programs aimed at rehabilitation. Second, the power to grant parole was thought to provide corrections officials with a tool for maintaining institutional control and discipline. The prospect of a reduced sentence in exchange for good behavior encouraged better conduct among inmates. Finally, release on parole, as a "back end" solution to prison crowding, was important from the beginning. For complete historical reviews, *see* Simon (1993) and Bottomly (1990).

Early Twentieth Century Parole: The Conflict Between Growth and Adaptation

The tremendous growth in parole as a concept, however, did not imply uniform development, public support, nor quality practices. As Bottomly writes, "it is doubtful whether parole ever really operated consistently in the United States either in principle or practice." Moreover, parole-as-rehabilitation was never taken very seriously, and from its inception, prison administrators used parole primarily to manage prison crowding and reduce inmate violence (Bottomly, 1990).

Despite its expanded usage, parole was controversial from the start (Rothman, 1980). A Gallup poll conducted in 1934 revealed that 82 percent of U.S. adults believed that parole was not strict enough and should not be granted as frequently (The Gallup Organization, 1998). Today, parole is still unpopular, and a recent survey shows that 80 percent of Americans favor making parole more difficult to obtain (The Gallup Organization, 1998). A comparable percentage is opposed to granting parole a second time to inmates who previously have been granted parole for a serious crime (Flanagan, 1996). On the other hand, the public significantly underestimates the amount of time inmates serve, so their lack of support for parole reflects that misperception (Flanagan, 1996).

Nonetheless, over time, the positivistic approach to crime and criminals—which viewed the offender as "sick" and in need of help—began to influence parole release and supervision. The rehabilitation ideal, as it came to be known, affected all of corrections well into the 1960s, and gained acceptance for the belief that the purpose of incarceration and parole was to change the offender's behavior rather than simply to punish. As Rhine (1996) notes, as the rehabilitative ideal evolved, indeterminate sentencing in tandem with parole acquired a newfound legitimacy. It also gave legitimacy and purpose to parole boards, which were supposed to be composed of "experts" in behavioral change, and it was their responsibility to discern that moment during confinement when the offender was rehabilitated and thus suitable for release.

Mid-twentieth Century Parole: The Conflict Between Release and Rehabilitation

Parole boards, usually political appointees, are given broad discretion to determine when an offender is ready for release—a decision limited only by the constraints of the maximum sentence imposed by the judge. Parole boards—usually composed of no more than ten individuals—also have the authority to rescind an established parole date, issue warrants and subpoenas, set conditions of supervision, restore offenders' civil rights, and grant final discharges. In most states, they also order the payment of restitution or supervision fees as a condition of parole release.

In the early years, there were few standards governing the decision to grant or deny parole, and decision-making rules were not made public. One of the long-standing criticisms of paroling authorities is that their members are too often selected based on party loyalty and political patronage, rather than professional qualifications and experience (Morse, 1939).

In *Conscience and Convenience*, David Rothman (1980) discusses the issue of discretionary decisions by parole boards. He reports that in the early twentieth century, parole boards considered primarily the seriousness of the crime in determining whether to release an inmate on parole. However, there was no consensus on what constituted a serious crime. Instead, according to Rothman, "each member made his own decisions. The judgments were personal and therefore not subject to debate or reconsideration" (Rothman, 1980:173). These personal preferences often resulted in unwarranted sentencing disparities or racial and gender bias (Tonry, 1995). As has been observed, "no other part of the criminal justice system concentrates such power in the hands of so few" (Rhine et al., 1991:32-33).

Regardless of criticisms, the use of parole release grew, and instead of using it as a special privilege to be extended to exceptional prisoners, it began to be used as a standard mode of release from prison, routinely considered upon completion of a minimum term of confinement. What had started as a practical alternative to executive clemency, and then came to be used as a mechanism for controlling prison growth, gradually developed a distinctively rehabilitative rationale, incorporating the promise of help, assistance, and surveillance (Bottomly, 1990:325).

By the mid-1950s, indeterminate sentencing coupled with parole release was well entrenched in the United States, such that it was the dominant sentencing structure in every state, and by the late 1970s, more than 70 percent of all inmates released were released as a result of a parole board discretionary decision. And in some states, essentially everyone was released as a result of the parole board's decisions. For example, throughout the 1960s, more than 95 percent of all inmates released in Washington, New Hampshire, and California were released on parole

(O'Leary, 1974). Indeterminate sentencing coupled with parole release was a matter of absolute routine and good correctional practice for most of the twentieth century. But all that was to change starting in the late 1970s, when demands for substantial reforms in parole practice increasingly began to be heard.

Modern Challenges and Changes to Parole

The pillars of the American corrections systems—indeterminate sentencing coupled with parole release, for the purposes of offender rehabilitation—came under severe attack and basically collapsed during the late 1970s and early 1980s. This period in penology has been well documented elsewhere and will not be repeated here. For an excellent review *see* Reitz, 1998.

In summary, attacks on indeterminate sentencing and parole release seem to have centered on three major criticisms. First, *there was little scientific evidence that parole release and supervision reduced subsequent recidivism.* In 1974, Robert Martinson and his colleagues published the now-famous review of the effectiveness of correctional treatment and concluded: "With few and isolated exceptions, the rehabilitative efforts that have been reported so far have had no appreciable effect on recidivism" (Lipton, Martinson, and Wilks, 1975). Of the 289 studies they reviewed, just 25 (8.6 percent) pertained to parole, and yet their summary was interpreted to mean that parole supervision (and all rehabilitation programs) did not work.

The National Research Council reviewed the Martinson data and basically concurred with the conclusions reached (Sechrest, White, and Brown, 1979). Martinson's study is often credited with giving rehabilitation the *coup de grace.* As Holt (1998) notes, once rehabilitation could not be legitimated by science, there was nothing to support the "readiness for release" idea, and, therefore, no role for parole boards or indeterminate sentencing.

Second, *parole and indeterminate sentencing were challenged on moral grounds as unjust and inhumane,* especially when imposed on unwilling participants. Research showed there was little relationship between in-prison behavior, participation in rehabilitation programs, and postrelease recidivism (Glaser, 1969). If that were true, then why base release dates on in-prison performance? Prisoners argued that not knowing their release dates held them in "suspended animation" and contributed one more pain of imprisonment.

Third, indeterminate sentencing permitted authorities to use a great deal of *uncontrolled discretion in release decisions, and these decisions often were inconsistent and discriminatory*. Since parole boards had a great deal of autonomy and their decisions were not subject to outside scrutiny, critics argued that it was a hidden system of discretionary decision making and led to race and class bias in release decisions (Citizens' Inquiry on Parole and Criminal Justice, 1974).

Three Sentencing Alternatives Proposed

It seemed as if no one liked indeterminate sentencing and parole in the early 1980s, and the time was ripe for change. Crime control advocates denounced parole supervision as being largely nominal and ineffective; social welfare advocates decried the lack of meaningful and useful rehabilitation programs. Several scholars, including James Q. Wilson, Andrew von Hirsch, and David Fogel, began to advocate alternative sentencing proposals.

Wilson argued that if there were no scientific basis for the possibility of rehabilitation, then the philosophical rationale for making it the chief goal of sentencing should be abandoned. He urged instead a revival of interest in the deterrence and incapacitation functions of the criminal justice system. He urged the abandonment of rehabilitation as a major purpose of corrections: "Instead we could view the correctional system as having a very different function—to isolate and to punish. That statement may strike many readers as cruel, even barbaric. It is not. It is merely recognition that society must be able to protect itself from dangerous offenders. . . . It is also a frank admission that society really does not know how to do much else" (Wilson, 1985:193).

Von Hirsch provided a seemingly neutral ideological substitute for rehabilitation (Holt, 1998). He argued that the discredited rehabilitation model should be replaced with a simple nonutilitarian notion that sentencing sanctions should reflect the social harm caused by the misconduct. Indeterminacy and parole should be replaced with a specific penalty for a specific offense. He believed that all persons committing the same crimes "deserve" to be sentenced to conditions that are similar in both type and duration, and that individual traits such as rehabilitation or the potential for recidivism should be irrelevant to the sentencing and parole decision. He proposed abolishing parole and adopting a system of "just deserts" sentencing, where similarly situated criminal conduct would be punished similarly (von Hirsch, 1976).

Fogel advocated for a "justice model" for prisons and parole, where inmates would be given opportunities to volunteer for rehabilitation programs, but that participation would not be required. He criticized the unbridled discretion exercised by correctional officials, particularly parole boards, under the guise of "treatment." He recommended a return to flat time/determinate sentencing and the elimination of parole boards. He also advocated abolishing parole's surveillance function and turning that function over to law enforcement (Fogel, 1975).

The Call to End Rehabilitation and Parole

These individuals had a major influence on both academic and policy thinking about sentencing objectives. Together, they advocated a system with less emphasis on rehabilitation, and the abolition of indeterminate sentencing and discretionary parole release. Liberals and conservatives endorsed the proposals. The political left was concerned about excessive discretion that permitted vastly different sentences in presumably similar cases, and the political right was concerned about the leniency of parole boards. A political coalition resulted, and soon incapacitation and "just deserts" replaced rehabilitation as the primary goal of American prisons.

With that changed focus, the indeterminate sentencing and parole release came under serious attack, and calls for "abolishing parole" were heard in state after state. In 1976, Maine became the first state to eliminate parole. The following year, California and Indiana joined Maine in establishing determinate sentencing legislation and abolishing discretionary parole release. As noted, by the end of 2000, fifteen states had abolished discretionary parole release for all inmates. In addition, in twenty-one states, parole authorities are operating under

TABLE 1: STATUS OF PAROLE RELEASE IN THE UNITED STATES, 2001

	Parole Board Has Full Release Powers	Parole Board Has Limited Release Powers	If Parole Board Powers Are Limited, Crimes Ineligible for Discretionary Release	Discretionary Parole Abolished (Year Abolished)
Alabama	✔			
Alaska		✔		
Arizona				✔ (1994)
Arkansas		✔		
California		✔	Only for indeterminate life sentences	
Colorado	✔			
Connecticut		✔	Murders, capital felonies	
Delaware				✔ (1990)
Florida		✔	Certain capital/life felonies	
Georgia		✔	Several felonies	
Hawaii		✔	Punishment by life without parole	
Idaho	✔			
Illinois				✔ (1978)
Indiana				✔ (1977)
Iowa		✔	Murder 1, kidnaping, sex abuse	
Kansas				✔ (1993)
Kentucky	✔			
Louisiana		✔	Several felonies	
Maine				✔ (1975)
Maryland		✔	Violent, or death penalty sought	
Massachusetts		✔	Murder 1	
Michigan		✔	Murder 1, 650+ grams cocaine	
Minnesota				✔ (1980)
Mississippi				✔ (1995)
Missouri		✔	Several felonies	
Montana	✔			
Nebraska		✔	Murder 1/life, kidnaping/life	
Nevada	✔			
New Hampshire		✔	Murder 1	
New Jersey	✔			
New Mexico				✔ (1979)
New York		✔	"Violent felony offenders"	
North Carolina				✔ (1994)
North Dakota	✔			
Ohio				✔ (1996)
Oklahoma	✔			
Oregon				✔ (1989)
Pennsylvania	✔			
Rhode Island	✔			
South Carolina	✔			
South Dakota		✔	None with life sentence	
Tennessee		✔	Murder 1/life, rapes	
Texas		✔	None on death row	
Utah	✔			
Vermont	✔			
Virginia				✔ (1995)
Washington				✔ (1984)
West Virginia		✔	No life without mercy	
Wisconsin		✔	No life without parole	
Wyoming	✔			
Total	15	21		14

Note: This information is from the National Institute of Corrections (1997) and updated with information from Ditton and Wilson (1999) and the author.

what might be called a sundown provision, in that they have discretion over a small or diminished parole-eligible population. Today, just fifteen states have given their parole boards full authority to release inmates through a discretionary process (*see* Table 1).

Likewise, at the federal level, the Comprehensive Crime Control Act of 1984 created the U.S. Sentencing Commission. That legislation abolished the U.S. Parole Commission, and parole was phased out from the federal criminal justice system in 1997. Offenders sentenced to federal prison, while no longer eligible for parole release, are now required to serve a defined term of "supervised release" following release from prison (Adams and Roth, 1998).

One of the presumed effects of eliminating parole or limiting its use is to increase the length of the prison term served. After all, parole release is widely regarded as "letting them out early." Time served in prison has increased in recent years, but it is attributed to the implementation of truth-in-sentencing laws, rather than the abolition of parole boards. The Bureau of Justice Statistics data reveal no obvious relationship between the type of release (mandatory versus parole board) and the actual length of time spent in prison prior to release. For all offense types combined, the mean (average) time served in prison for those released from state prison in 1996 through "discretionary" (parole) methods was twenty-five months served; whereas for those released "mandatorily," the average (mean) time served in prison was twenty-four months (Ditton and Wilson, 1999). Allen Beck, chief of corrections statistics at the Bureau of Justice Statistics, recently observed that ending parole by itself "has had no real impact on time served" (Butterfield, 1999:11).

"Three Strikes" and "Truth-in-Sentencing" Reform Laws: Parole Today

Offenders, however, are spending greater amounts of time in prison and on parole. These longer time periods may make it more difficult for offenders to maintain family contacts and other social supports, thereby contributing to their social isolation upon release. As Table 2 shows, the average (mean) time served among released state prisoners, for all types of offenders, has increased from an

TABLE 2: TIME SERVED IN PRISON, JAIL, AND ON PAROLE: ALL OFFENSE TYPES COMBINED, IN MONTHS

	1985	1990	1996	1999
Average time served in jail	6	6	5	5
Average time served in prison	20	22	25	29
Time served on parole	19	22	23	26
Total months	45	50	53	60

Source: Data from the Bureau of Justice Statistics, *National Corrections Reporting Program*, 1985, 1990, 1996; Bureau of Justice Statistics, Trends in State Parole, 1990-2000. Includes only offenders with a sentence of more than one year released for the first time on the current sentence. Time served on parole is for "successful" exits.

average of twenty months in 1985 to twenty-nine months in 1999. The median prison term served has increased from fourteen months in 1985 to fifteen months in 1996. Similarly, the length of time on parole supervision (for those successfully discharged) has increased, from an average of nineteen months in 1985 to twenty-six months in 1999. The average time on parole for "unsuccessful exits" was nineteen months in 1985, and twenty-one months in 1996 (Bureau of Justice Statistics, 1998; Hughes, Wilson, and Beck, 2001).

Even in states that did not formally abolish parole or restrict its use to certain serious offenses, the sentencing reform movement produced a significant diminution of parole boards' discretionary authority to release. Mandatory minimum-sentencing policies now exist in every state, and the federal government and twenty-five states have enacted "three strikes and you're out" laws that require extremely long minimum terms for certain repeat offenders (Lyons, 2000).

Perhaps most significantly, twenty-nine states and the District of Columbia have established "truth-in-sentencing" laws, under which people convicted of selected violent crimes must serve at least 85 percent of the announced prison sentence. To satisfy the 85 percent test (to qualify for federal funds for prison construction), states have limited the powers of parole boards to set release dates, or of prison managers to award good time and gain time (time off for good behavior or for participation in work or treatment programs), or both. As a result, violent offenders' postrelease oversight time has decreased to 15 percent of the imposed sentence (Travis, 2000). Truth-in-sentencing laws not only effectively eliminate parole but also most "good time" (Ditton and Wilson, 1999).

Even in the fifteen jurisdictions that give parole authorities discretion to release, most of them use formal risk prediction instruments (or parole guidelines) to assist in parole decision making (Runda, Rhine, and Wetter, 1994). *Parole guidelines* are usually actuarial devices, which objectively predict the risk of recidivism based on crime and offender background information. The guidelines produce a "seriousness" score for each individual by summing points assigned for various background characteristics (higher scores mean greater risk). Inmates with the least serious crime and the lowest statistical probability of reoffending would then be the first to be released and so forth. The use of such objective instruments helps to reduce the disparity in parole release decision making, and has been shown to be more accurate than release decisions based on the case study or individualized method (Holt, 1998). One half of U.S. jurisdictions now use formal risk assessment instruments in relation to parole release (Runda, Rhine, and Wetter, 1994).

CHAPTER FOUR

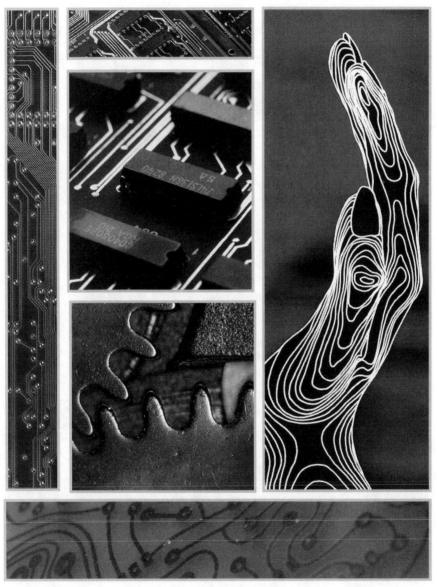

Characteristics of the Current Parole
Population

Number of Parolees under Supervision

While discretionary parole release has declined, parole supervision remains in almost every state. And, as the size of the prison populations has risen, so too has the parole population. The Bureau of Justice Statistics reports that, at year end 2000, there were 652,199 adults on parole in the United States. Persons on parole represented 10 percent of the approximate 6.5 million persons who were "under correctional control" (incarcerated or on community supervision) at year end 2000 (Hughes, Wilson, and Beck, 2001; Bureau of Justice Statistics, 2001b).

The growth in parole populations has slowed considerably in recent years, increasing just 2.3 percent in 1999, after growing 24 percent between 1990-1992. The number of parolees continues to increase at an average annual rate of 0.7 percent (Bureau of Justice Statistics, 2000; Hughes, Wilson, and Beck, 2001). This is the smallest growth of any of the correctional populations, and likely reflects a short-term lull in the growth of the parole population, primarily as a consequence of an increase in the average length of prison terms being served as a result of truth-in-sentencing policies (Ditton and Wilson, 1999).

Over half (64 percent) of all persons on parole in the United States were in California, New York, Pennsylvania or Texas. California led the nation with 117,647 adults on parole in 2000, followed by Texas with 111,719. Between 1990 and 2000, however, the parole population in Texas increased by only 6.7 percent, while the California population increased by 72.7 percent (Hughes, Wilson, and Beck, 2001). The District of Columbia has, by far, the greatest percentage of its resident population on parole supervision. In 2000, nearly 1.2 percent of all its residents were on parole supervision, compared to a national average of .03 percent (Bureau of Justice Statistics, 2001b).

Selected Characteristics of Parolees

As noted earlier, there is little available information on the characteristics of persons on parole. The Bureau of Justice Statistics reports some basic characteristics of those entering parole as part of its *National Corrections Reporting Program* series. They also reported similar data in "Trends of State Parole, 1990-2000." In 2000, similar to other correctional populations, males constituted most of the parolee population (90 percent), although the percentage of female parolees increased from 8 percent in 1990 to 10 percent in 2000. Of the parole population, 35 percent were white and 47 percent were black, while 16 percent were of Hispanic origin (Hughes, Wilson, and Beck, 2001). The mean age of the total parolee population was thirty-four years, and almost half were high school graduates, and 11 percent of parolees had an education level below the eighth grade, and an additional 40 percent were at an educational level between the ninth and eleventh grade level (Hughes, Wilson, and Beck, 2001). These characteristics have remained fairly constant since the early 1980s.

The only parolee characteristic that has changed in recent years appears to be conviction crime. In 1988, 30 percent of first entries to parole were convicted of violence, but in 1999, that figure had dropped to 24 percent. In 1985, just 12 percent of those persons released to parole were convicted of drug crimes, whereas in 1999, that was true for 35 percent of first releases to parole (Beck, 1999; Hughes, Wilson, and Beck, 2001). More than a third of all entrants to parole were convicted of drug-related crimes (*see* Table 3). Federal offenders also reflect this trend: in 1999, 27 percent of parolees had been violent offenders, while almost 52 percent had committed a drug offense (Bureau of Justice Statistics, 2001a).

Individual states sometimes publish descriptions of their parolees. For example, a report by the California Parole and Community Services Division reported the following (California Department of Corrections, 1997):

- 85 percent of parolees were chronic substance abusers (almost 40 percent drug offenders, according to the California website in 2001).

- 10 percent were homeless, but homelessness is as high as 30 to 50 percent among parolees in San Francisco and Los Angeles.

TABLE 3: CONVICTION OFFENSES OF PERSONS ENTERING PAROLE, SELECTED YEARS (IN PERCENT)

Most Serious Offense	First Entries to Parole Supervision				
	1988	1990	1992	1994	1996
Violent offenses	30.1	25.2	25.5	23.5	23.6
Homicide	3.8	3.0	2.7	2.3	2.1
Sexual Assault	5.4	4.2	4.2	4.4	4.3
Robbery	13.7	11.2	10.7	8.7	8.9
Assault	6.3	5.8	6.6	6.9	6.9
Other violent offenses	.9	1.0	1.0	1.2	1.4
Property offenses	42.2	37.2	32.7	33.3	31.0
Burglary	20.8	17.5	14.8	14.5	12.9
Larceny/theft	10.2	9.6	8.4	8.5	8.1
Motor vehicle theft	2.9	2.7	2.7	3.1	2.7
Fraud	5.1	4.6	3.9	4.2	4.3
Other propertyoffenses	3.2	2.8	2.9	3.0	3.0
Drug offenses	19.2	28.2	31.1	31.6	34.7
Possession	6.0	8.6	8.2	7.0	10.0
Trafficking	10.4	15.6	19.3	19.5	19.5
Other	2.8	4.0	3.6	5.1	5.2
Public-order offense:	7.1	8.1	9.8	10.5	10.1
Weapons	1.9	1.8	2.2	2.4	2.7
DWI/DUI	N.A.	3.0	3.7	3.5	3.2
Other	N.A.	3.3	3.9	4.6	4.2
Other offenses	1.4	1.3	1.2	1.1	.6

- 70 to 90 percent of all parolees were unemployed.

- 50 percent were functionally illiterate. More than one-half of all parolees read below the sixth grade level and therefore, could not fill out job applications or compete in the job market.

- 18 percent have some sort of psychiatric problem.

California's parole population clearly illustrates the need for far-reaching social programs to help rehabilitate offenders as they reenter mainstream society.

CHAPTER FIVE

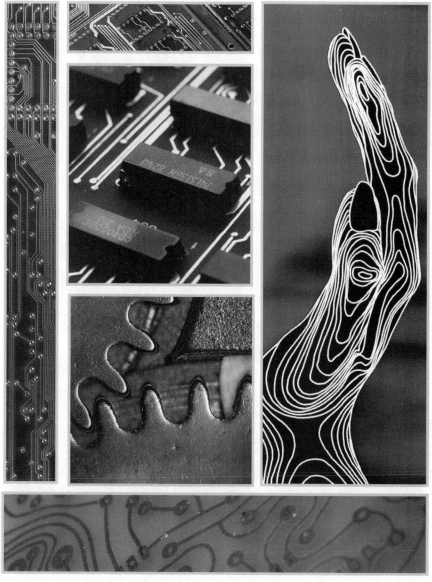

The Reentry Process and
Parole Supervision

Administration of Parole Field Services

As noted earlier, parole consists of two parts: *parole boards*, which have the authority to decide when to release prisoners, and *parole field services*, whose parole officers supervise offenders after their release. The major criticisms of parole release (for example, lack of professionalism, unwarranted discretion, and ineffectiveness) also were leveled at field supervision, and caused major changes and reforms there, as well.

One of the first and continuing reforms in parole field services has been to make them more independent of parole boards. Since the mid-1960s, states increasingly have moved parole field services away from being an arm of the parole board, and into a separate agency. According to the American Correctional Association, the parole field service agency is housed under a separate agency in forty states (80 percent), usually in the state's department of corrections. Parole boards have responsibility for supervising parolees in only ten states (20 percent) (American Correctional Association, 2000).

Regardless of their administrative relationship, parole board directives heavily influence how parole agents carry out their duties and responsibilities. When setting the conditions of release, parole boards, in fact, are prescribing the goals it expects parole agents to pursue in the period of supervision. A 1999 survey by the Association of Paroling Authorities, International (APAI) shows that most parole boards are responsible for ordering community service, restitution, supervision fees, sex offender registration, and treatment program participation (2000). In addition, some parole boards also mandate drug testing, intensified supervision (such as the lifetime supervision of sex offenders in Colorado and of child molesters in Rhode Island), and participation in victim mediation programs.

In most states, the decision to revoke parole ultimately rests with the parole board. There are exceptions: in Maryland, only the governor can grant parole to a prisoner with a life sentence. In Oklahoma, the governor ultimately makes all final parole decisions (American Correctional Association, 2001a). As such, parole boards set implicit and explicit criteria about which types of parole violations will warrant return to prison, and, as such, heavily influence the types of behavior parole officers monitor and record. If, for example, failing a drug test is not a violation that will result in revocation to prison or any serious consequence by the parole board, parole agents will not administer drug tests as frequently, since no consequence can be guaranteed (McCleary, 1992). In this way, parole boards and parole field services are functionally interdependent.

Offenders' Needs for Services Versus Parole's Supervisory Control

Persons released from prison face a multitude of difficulties in trying to reenter the outside community successfully. They remain largely uneducated, unskilled, and usually without solid family support systems—and now they have the added burden of a prison record and the distrust and fear that it inevitably elicits. Most have a substance abuse history, and one in six suffer from mental illness (Travis, Solomon, and Waul, 2001). If they are African-American and under the age of thirty, they join the largest group of unemployed in the country, with the added handicap of former convict status (Clear and Cole, 1997). As Irwin and Austin write: "Any imprisonment reduces the opportunities of felons, most of whom had relatively few opportunities to begin with" (1994:133).

Research has shown that parolees want the same things in life as the rest of us, although most believe they will not succeed (Richards, 1995). Most aspire to a relatively modest, stable, conventional life after prison. "When I get out, I want to have my kids with me and have a good job so I can support them" (Irwin and Austin, 1994:126).

The public, too, would like them to succeed. But what assistance are parolees given as they reenter our communities? Sadly, while inmates' need for services and assistance has increased, parole in some states (if not most) has retreated from its historical mission to provide counseling, job training, and housing assistance. Between 1990 and 1998, the percentage of inmates released by parole boards (with supervision and services) has steadily decreased; meanwhile, the percentage of mandatory releases and unconditional releases (with little or no such support) has steadily increased (Travis, Solomon, and Waul, 2001).

An excellent ethnographic study of parole officers in California concludes that while "rehabilitation" remains in parole's rhetoric, as a practical matter, parole services are almost entirely focused on control-oriented activities (Lynch, 1998). Agents have constructed an image of the prototypical parolee as someone who generally chooses to maintain an involvement with crime, and who needs no more than an attitude adjustment to get on the "right track," and who does not need the agent to provide intervention and services to facilitate reform. As Lynch observes: "In this way, while parole may talk of the need and capability for reform among their clientele, the agency can absolve itself of the responsibility to provide it" (Lynch, 1998:857). Even when traditional rehabilitative tools are available to agents—for example, drug treatment and counseling—they "are treated as rehabilitative in discourse, but are often used for coercive control in practice" (Lynch, 1998:860).

Parole Services

Of course, what help parolees receive differs vastly depending on the state and jurisdiction in which they are being supervised. But as states put more and more of their fiscal resources into building prisons, fewer resources are available for parole services. Oklahoma senators estimate that the state pays $36 million annually to incarcerate parole candidates, half of whom are on waiting lists to enter rehabilitation programs required by their parole conditions (Hinton, 2001). And, as noted earlier, the public has become less tolerant and forgiving of past criminal transgressions, and more fearful of particular offenders (for example, sex offenders). This sentiment has been translated into both stricter requirements for release, and stricter supervision and revocation procedures once released.

In California, for example, there are few services for parolees. There are only 200 shelter beds in the state for more than 10,000 homeless parolees, 4 mental health clinics for 18,000 psychiatric cases, 750 beds in treatment programs for 85,000 drug and alcohol abusers (Little Hoover Commission, 1998). Under the terms of their parole, offenders are often subjected to periodic drug tests. But they are rarely offered any opportunity to get drug treatment. Of the approximately 130,000 substance abusers in California's prisons, only 3,000 are receiving treatment behind bars. And of the 132,000 inmates released last year in California, just 8,000 received any kind of prerelease program to help them cope with life on the outside. As was recently reported:

> Inmates are simply released from prison each year in California, given nothing more than $200 and a bus ticket back to the county where they were convicted. At least 1,200 inmates every year go from a secure housing unit at a Level 4 prison—an isolation unit, designed to hold the most violent and dangerous inmates in the system—right onto the street. One day these predatory inmates are locked in their cells for twenty-three hours at a time and fed all their meals through a slot in the door, and the next day they're out of prison, riding a bus home (Schlosser, 1998:51).

The national picture is almost as disturbing. The Office of National Drug Control Policy (ONDCP) recently reported that 70 to 85 percent of state prison inmates need substance abuse treatment; however, just 13 percent will receive any kind of treatment while incarcerated (McCaffrey, 1998). Indeed, almost 14 percent of parole violators are incarcerated for drug-related violations (Beck, 2000).

Parole Conditions

All parolees are required to sign an agreement to abide by certain regulations. Seeing that the parolee lives up to this parole contract is the principal responsibility of the parole agent. Parole agents are equipped with legal authority to carry and use firearms, to search places, persons, and property without the requirements imposed by the Fourth Amendment (in other words, the right to privacy), and to order arrests without probable cause and to confine without bail. The power to search applies to the household where a parolee is living and businesses where a parolee is working. The ability to arrest, confine, and, in some cases, reimprison the parolee for violating conditions of agreement makes the parole agent a walking court system (Rudovsky et al., 1988).

Conditions generally can be grouped into standard conditions applicable to all parolees and special conditions that are tailored to particular offenders. Special conditions for substance abusers, for example, usually include periodic drug testing. Standard conditions are similar throughout most jurisdictions, and violating them can result in a return to prison. Common standard parole conditions include the following:

- Reporting to the parole agent within twenty-four hours of release

- Not carrying weapons

- Reporting changes of address and employment

- Not traveling more than fifty miles from home or not leaving the county for more than forty-eight hours without prior approval from the parole agent

- Obeying all parole agent instructions

- Seeking and maintaining employment, or participating in education/work training

- Not committing crimes.

- Submitting to search by the police and parole officers

Some argue that we have created unrealistic parole conditions. Boards were asked in 1988 to indicate from a list of fourteen items which were standard parole conditions in their state. The most common, of course, was "obey all laws." However, 78 percent required "gainful employment" as a standard condition; 61 percent required "no association with persons with criminal records;" 53 percent required "all fines and restitution paid;" and 47 percent required "support family and all dependents," none of which can consistently be met by most parolees (Rhine et al., 1991). Increasingly, the most common condition for probationers and parolees is drug testing. In 1998, almost half of the states' parole agencies tested almost 2.1 million parolees for drugs, and almost 1 percent were revoked (Camp and Camp, 2000). More than half of the parole systems the American Correctional Association surveyed reported the following factors for parole revocation: failing to report, ignoring stipulated programs, possessing a weapon, leaving the area without permission, and failing to secure or hold a job (American Correctional Association, 2001a).

Striking a Balance Between Services and Supervision

In October, 1998, the State of Maryland began ordering every drug addict released on parole or probation to report for urine tests twice a week in an ambitious attempt to force about 25,000 criminals statewide to undergo drug treatment or face a series of quick, escalating punishments. The project, known as "Break the Cycle," is based on the theory that frequent drug testing coupled with swift, graduated punishments for drug use will force more addicts off drugs than the threat of long jail terms or treatment programs alone ever could. The state anticipates that more than a million tests annually may be required to make the plan work, compared with the 40,000 tests the state administered in 1997 (Pan, 1998).

The Massachusetts reentry court pilot program is another example of targeting drug-abusing release candidates. Boston's experimental program starts rehabilitating and monitoring candidates ninety days before release. The former inmates continue receiving counseling, substance abuse treatment, and community support after release. The U.S. Attorney General's office predicted that Boston's program, used to monitor some of the 15,000 annual releases, would serve as a model for other cities (*Corrections Digest*, 2000). Other reentry court pilot projects—which target specific high-risk offenders and use court and parole office collaboration to help set goals for offenders—have been established in Colorado, Delaware, Florida, Kentucky, and New York (National Institute of Justice, 2000).

Parole Classification

When parolees first report to the parole field office, they usually are interviewed to be classified and assigned to a caseload. Most jurisdictions rely on a formal approach to classification and case management for parolee supervision. Such systems recognize that not all offenders are equal in their need for supervision. A recent parole survey found that 90 percent of the states use a classification system for assigning parolees to different levels of supervision (Runda, Rhine, and Wetter, 1994).

Most often, this assignment is based on a structured assessment of parolee risk, and an assessment of the needs or problem areas that have contributed to the parolee's criminality. By scoring information relative to the risk of recidivism, and the particular needs of the offender (in other words, a risk/need instrument) a total score is derived, which then dictates the particular level of parole supervision (for example, intensive, medium, minimum, administrative). Each jurisdiction usually has established policy that dictates the contact levels (times the officer will meet with the parolee). These contact levels correspond to each level of parole supervision. The notion is that higher risk inmates and those with greater needs will be seen most frequently (for example, on "intensive" caseloads). These models are described as "management tools," and are not devised to reduce recidivism directly (Holt, 1998).

Specialized Caseloads

Larger parole departments also have established "specialized caseloads" to supervise certain types of offenders more effectively. These offenders generally pose a particularly serious threat to public safety or present unique problems that may handicap their adjustment to supervision. Specialized caseloads afford the opportunity to match the unique skills and training of parole officers with the specialized needs of parolees. The most common specialized caseloads in the United States are those that target sex offenders and parolees with serious substance abuse problems, although as shown in Table 4, fewer than 4 percent of all parolees are supervised on specialized caseloads.

Caseload Assignment

Cases are then assigned to parole officers and comprise officers' caseloads. Table 4 contains the latest information on these characteristics for U.S. parolees.

TABLE 4: PAROLE CASELOAD SUPERVISION LEVEL, CONTACTS, AND ANNUAL COSTS

Caseload Type	Percent of All Parolees	Average Caseload Size	Face to Face Contacts	Annual Supervision Costs
Regular	85.1	66:1	21/year	$1,806
Intensive	13.6	25:1	68/year	$4,114
Electronic monitoring	1.1	13:1	42/year	$5,716
Specialized	3.1	32:1	50/year	$4,938

Source: Camp and Camp (2000).

Table 4 shows that more than 80 percent of U.S. parolees are supervised on regular caseloads, averaging sixty-seven cases to one parole officer, in which they are seen (face to face) less than twice per month. Officers also may conduct "collateral" contacts, such as contacting family members or employers to inquire about the parolee's progress. Many parole officers are frustrated because they lack the time and resources to do the kind of job they believe is maximally helpful to their clients. Parole officers often complain that paperwork has increased, their clients have more serious problems, and that their caseloads are much higher than the thirty-five to fifty cases that have been considered the ideal caseload for a parole officer. However, there is no empirical evidence to show that smaller caseloads result in lower recidivism rates (Petersilia and Turner, 1993).

One important implication of larger caseloads and the reduction in the quality of client supervision is the increased potential for lawsuits arising from negligent supervision by parole officer's clients (del Carmen and Pilant, 1994). In a 1986 Alaska case, the Alaska Supreme Court ruled that state agencies and their officers may be held liable for negligence when probationers and parolees under their supervision commit violent offenses (*Division of Corrections v. Neakok*, 1986). Thus, parole officers are increasingly at risk through tort actions filed by victims harmed by the crimes committed by their offender-clients. Some have argued that this legal threat eventually forces states to invest more heavily in parole supervision.

Violations of Conditions and Parole Revocation

If parolees fail to live up to their conditions, they can be revoked to custody. Parole can be revoked for two reasons: (1) the commission of a new crime or (2)

the violation of the conditions of parole (a "technical violation"). Technical violations pertain to behavior that is not criminal, such as the failure to refrain from alcohol use or remain employed.

In either event, the violation process is rather straightforward. Given that parolees are technically still in the legal custody of the prison or parole authorities, and as a result maintain a quasiprisoner status, their constitutional rights are severely limited. When parole officers become aware of violations of the parole contract, they notify their supervisors, who rather easily can return a parolee to prison.

Parole revocations are an administrative function that is typically devoid of court involvement. However, parolees do have some rights in revocation proceedings. Two U.S. Supreme Court cases, *Morrissey v. Brewer* (1972), and *Gagnon v. Scarpelli* (1973) are considered landmark cases of parolee rights in revocation proceedings. Among other things, *Morrissey* and *Gagnon* established minimum requirements for the revocation of parole boards, forcing boards to conform to some standards of due process. Parolees must be given written notice of the nature of the violation and the evidence obtained, and they have a right to confront and cross-examine their accusers.

Changing Nature of Parole Supervision and Services

Historically, parole agents were viewed as paternalistic figures that mixed authority with help. Officers provided direct services (for example, counseling) and also knew the community and brokered services (for example, job training) to needy offenders. As noted earlier, parole was originally designed to make the transition from prison to the community more gradual and, during this time, parole officers were to assist the offender in addressing personal problems and searching for employment and a place to live. Many parole agencies still do assist in these "service" activities. Increasingly, however, parole supervision has shifted away from providing services to parolees, and more toward providing monitoring and surveillance activities such as drug testing, monitoring curfews, and collecting restitution.

A recent survey of twenty-one parole agencies shows that fourteen provide job development help, eight offer detoxification services, and twelve offer substance abuse treatment, yet all do drug testing (Camp and Camp, 2000). Historically, offering "services" and treatment to parolees was commonplace, but such services are dwindling.

There are a number of reasons for this shift. For one, a greater number of parole conditions are being assigned to released prisoners. In the federal system, for example, between 1987 and 1996, the proportion of offenders required to comply with at least one special supervision condition increased from 67 percent of entrants to 91 percent (Adams and Roth, 1998). Parolees in state systems also are being required to submit more frequently to drug testing, complete community service, and make restitution payments (Petersilia and Turner, 1993).

Parole officers work for the corrections system, and if paroling authorities are imposing a greater number of conditions on parolees, then field agents must monitor those conditions. As a result, contemporary parole officers have less time to provide other services, such as counseling, even if they were inclined to do so.

Economic Difficulty of Maintaining Parole Supervision and Services

It is also true that the fiscal crisis experienced in most states has reduced the number of treatment and job training programs in the community-at-large, and given the fear and suspicion surrounding ex-convicts, these persons usually are placed at the end of the waiting lists. The ability to "broker" services to parolees, given the scarcity of programs, has become increasingly difficult. If there is one common complaint among parole officers in the United States, it is the lack of available treatment and job programs for parolees. At the end of the 1960s, when the country had more employment opportunities for blue collar workers than it does now, there was some movement to reduce the employment barriers, and studies revealed a full-time employment rate of around 50 percent for parolees (Simon, 1993). Today, full-time employment among parolees is rare (Uggen, 2000).

The main reason, however, that "services" are not delivered to most parolees is that parole supervision has been transformed ideologically from a social service to a law enforcement system. Just as the prison system responded to the public's demands for accountability and justice, so did parole officers.

"Rehabilitation" Versus "Surveillance"

Feely and Simon (1992) argue that over the past few decades, a systems analysis approach to danger management has come to dominate parole, and it has evolved into a "waste management" system, rather than one focused on rehabilitation. In their model, those in the dangerous class of criminals are nearly synonymous with those in the larger social category of the underclass, a segment of the population that has been abandoned to a fate of poverty and despair. They suggest that a "new penology" has emerged, one that simply strives to manage risk by use of actuarial methods. Offenders are addressed not as individuals but as aggregate populations. The traditional correctional objectives of rehabilitation and the reduction of offender recidivism have given way to the rational and efficient deployment of control strategies for managing (and confining) high-risk criminals. Surveillance and control have replaced treatment as the main goals of parole.

Newly hired parole officers often embrace the "surveillance" versus "rehabilitation" model of parole, along with the quasipolicing role that parole has taken on in some locales. Twenty years ago, social work was the most common educational path for those pursuing careers in parole. Today, the most common educational path is criminal justice studies—an academic field spawned in the 1960s to professionalize law enforcement (Parent, 1993). Parole agents began to carry concealed firearms in the 1980s. Firearms are now provided in most jurisdictions and represent a major investment of training resources, agent time, and administrative oversight (Holt, 1998).

The programming innovations likewise represent a theme of control and supervision rather than service and assistance. Parolees are held more accountable for a broader range of behavior, including alcohol and substance abuse, restitution, curfews, and community service.

As Irwin and Austin (1994:129) put it: "Instead of helping prisoners locate a job, find a residence, or locate needed drug treatment serves, the new parole system is bent on surveillance and detection. Parolees are routinely and randomly checked for illegal drug use, failure to locate or maintain a job, moving without permission, or any other number of petty and nuisance-type behaviors that don't conform to the rules of parole."

In addition to the limitations set out in the parole contract and enforced by the parole officer, parolees face a growing number of legal restrictions or "civil disabilities." Ironically, these civil disabilities often restrict the parolees' ability to carry out one of the most common parole requirements—that of remaining employed. The next section reviews the most common restrictions.

Civil Disabilities and Injunctions of Convicted Felons

While the services available to assist parolees have decreased, the structural obstacles concerning their behavior have increased. Under federal law and the laws of many states, a felony conviction has consequences that continue long after a sentence has been served and parole has ended. For example, convicted felons lose essential rights of citizenship, such as the right to vote and to hold public office, and they may be restricted in their ability to obtain occupational and professional licenses. Their criminal record also may preclude them from retaining their parental rights, be grounds for divorce, and they may be barred from serving on a jury, holding public office, and owning firearms. These statutory restrictions or "civil disabilities" serve as punishments in addition to the conviction and sentence imposed by the court.

A recent survey shows that after a period where states were becoming less restrictive of convicted felons' rights, the effect of the "get tough movement" of the 1980s was to increase the statutory restrictions placed on parolees. Between 1986 and 1996, state legal codes revealed an increase in the extent to which states restricted the rights and opportunities available to released inmates (Olivares, Burton, and Cullen, 1996).

A complete state-by-state survey (Love and Kuzma, 1996) of civil disabilities of convicted felons, including parolees, included the following:

- *Right to Vote.* Fourteen states permanently deny convicted felons the right to vote, whereas most others temporarily restrict this right until the sentence has been fulfilled. Thirty-two states suspend the right to vote until the offender has completed the imposed sentence of parole (and paid all fines). Colorado is an example of a state where the "right to vote is lost if incarcerated, and automatically restored upon completion of sentence, including parole." California denies the right to vote to incarcerated offenders and parolees, yet allows probationers to vote. Allard and Mauer (2000) estimate that 1.4 million black males, or 13.1 percent of the black male adult population, are currently or permanently not able to vote as a result of a felony conviction. While most states have procedures for regaining the right to vote, it often requires a gubernatorial pardon.

- *Parental Rights.* Nineteen states may terminate the parental rights of convicted felons, if it can be shown that a felony conviction suggests a parent's unfitness to supervise or care for the child. Oregon and Tennessee require that the parent be incarcerated for a specified length of time (three years in Oregon, and two years in Tennessee).

- *Divorce.* The use of a felony conviction to permit divorce exists in nineteen states. In twenty-nine jurisdictions, a felony conviction constitutes legal grounds for divorce. In 1996, ten states considered any felony conviction as sufficient grounds, whereas seven jurisdictions require a felony conviction and imprisonment to grant a divorce.

- *Public Employment.* Public employment is permanently denied in six states: Alabama, Delaware, Iowa, Mississippi, Rhode Island, and South Carolina. The remaining jurisdictions permit public employment in varying degrees. Of these states, ten leave the decision to hire at the discretion of the employer, while twelve jurisdictions apply a "direct relationship test" to determine whether the conviction offense bears directly on the job in question. But the courts have interpreted the "direct relationship" standard liberally. For example, a California case (*Golde v. Fox*) found that conviction of possession of marijuana for sale was substantially related to the business of a real estate broker as it shows lack of honesty and integrity.

Each state has its own particular professions that have been restricted to ex-convicts. In Colorado, for example, the professions of dentist, engineer, nurse, pharmacist, physician, and realtor are closed to convicted felons. In California, the professions of law, real estate, medicine, nursing, physical therapy, and education are restricted. In

Virginia, the professions of optometry, nursing, dentistry, accounting, funeral directing, and pharmacist generally are closed to ex-felons.

- *Right to Serve as a Juror.* The right to serve as a juror is restricted permanently in thirty-two jurisdictions, and the remaining twenty states permit the right with consideration given to varying conditions. For example, ten states restrict the right only during sentence, while four jurisdictions impose an additional delay after sentence completion (for example, from one year in the District of Columbia to ten years in Kansas). As of 1999, only ex-convicts in the states of Colorado, Illinois, Iowa, Maine, and New Hampshire could serve on juries.

- *Right to Hold Public Office.* Seven states permanently deny elected office to persons convicted of specific crimes, including bribery, perjury, and embezzlement. Twenty states restrict the right to hold public office until the offender has completed his or her sentence of prison, probation, or parole. With the exceptions of Alaska and Vermont, all states restrict convicted felons who wish to hold public office.

- *Right to Own a Firearm.* Thirty-one of fifty-one jurisdictions permanently deny or restrict the right to own or posses a firearm on "any" felony conviction. In contrast, eighteen states deny the right to own or possess a firearm only for convictions involving violence.

- *Criminal Registration.* In 1986, only eight of fifty-one jurisdictions required offenders to register with a law enforcement agency upon release from prison. By 1998, every state required convicted sex offenders to register with law enforcement on release (Lieb, Quinsey, and Berliner, 1998). These state-registration schemes, so-called "Megan's Laws," vary considerably with respect to the crimes for which registration is required, the duration of the registration requirement, and the penalty for failure to register. Illinois, for example, requires sex offenders and those convicted of first-degree murder against a victim under eighteen years old to register. The registration typically lasts for a period of several years, but may extend for the life of the offender for certain crimes. In addition, California now requires sex offenders to provide blood and saliva samples for DNA testing, which can now be used as evidence for sex offense prosecution (National Conference of State Legislatures, 2001).

Jonathan Simon (1993) notes that these civil disabilities have the effect of creating an inherent contradiction in our legal system. He writes that different laws may serve different purposes, but they must not contradict one another. Yet, in the United States, we spend millions of dollars to "rehabilitate" offenders and convince them that they need to obtain legitimate employment, and then frustrate whatever was thereby accomplished by raising legal barriers that may bar them *absolutely* from employment and its rewards. He also notes that forced structural changes in the United States have taken their toll on the very population from which most parolees come, which, in turn, have impacted agents' ability to do their job. Most notably, the loss of a solid industrial base over the past few decades, which has traditionally supplied jobs among poorer inner-city communities, has left urban parolees with few opportunities, and left agents with fewer venues in which to monitor and supervise their clients (Lynch, 1998).

CHAPTER SIX

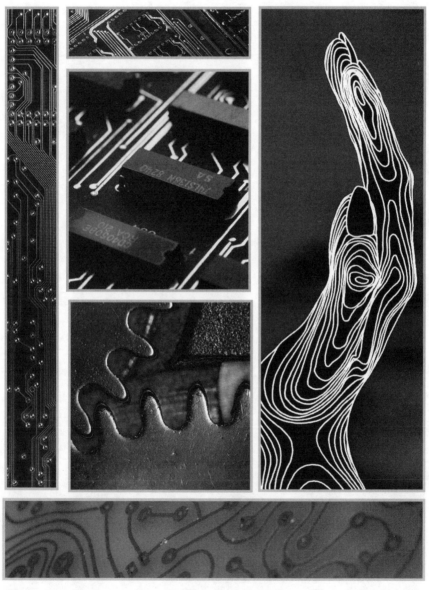

Parole Outcomes: Completion, Recidivism,
and Parolee Contribution to Crime

The most common question asked about parole is, "Does it work?" And, by "work" most mean do persons granted parole refrain from further crime or reduce their "recidivism." Recidivism is currently the primary outcome measure for parole, as it is for all corrections programs.

Prisoner Recidivism Rates

The most comprehensive study of state prisoner recidivism tracked 16,000 inmates released during 1983 in eleven states. The study found that, overall, 63 percent of inmates were arrested for a felony or serious misdemeanor offense within three years of release from prison. In unpublished data from that cohort, Beck reports that 62.3 percent of those who were released "conditionally" (in other words, on parole) were rearrested within three years, whereas the figure was 64.8 percent for those who were released "unconditionally." About 47 percent of inmates were convicted of a new offense during the three years after release, and 41 percent returned to prison or jail for a new offense or technical violation of their prison release (Beck and Shipley, 1989).

The Beck and Shipley study is the best available to approximate the recidivism rates of parolees, but it has some limitations. Not all persons released from prison were officially on parole; however, in the early 1980s most were, so that this data captures most parolee recidivism. Also, the study tracked inmates for a full three-year period after release, and offenders may or may not have been officially on parole for all of that time period. The study was also conducted more than eighteen years ago, and we know that parole policy has changed considerably since that time.

The Bureau of Justice Statistics maintains records of the numbers of parole violators sentenced to state prisons (up to 206,751 in 1998) (Bureau of Justice

Statistics, 2000). The Association of Paroling Authorities, International, updated the Parole Board Survey in 1999, providing state-by-state totals of violation hearings, revocations, and successful discharges (New York alone discharged 15,612 parolees to discretionary release in 1999). In 2001, the American Correctional Association surveyed 39 parole systems who reported successful annual completion rates as low as around 20 percent (in Idaho, Ohio, and Pennsylvania) and as high as 90 percent in Florida (American Correctional Association, 2001a). However, there is no definitive study that computes recidivism rates of parolees.

Successful Versus Unsuccessful Completion of Parole

The Bureau of Justice Statistics, as part of its *National Corrections Reporting Program*, collects data each year from every state about its parole population, and how many of its parolees have successfully completed parole. This data derives from parole agency records, not from the police, and hence it may not capture all arrests. It is possible, for example, for an offender to be arrested (say, for a misdemeanor or low level felony) and not be violated from parole, and hence this is recorded as a "successful exit" from parole.

FIGURE 2: STATE PAROLE OUTCOMES, 1985-1999

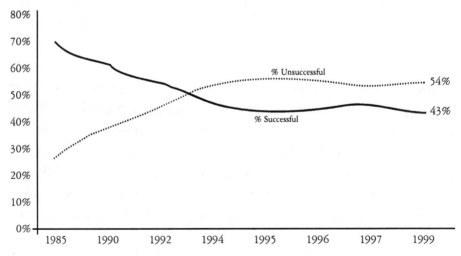

Sources: Bureau of Justice Statistics, *Annual Parole Survey*, 1981, 1986-1997, "U.S. Correctional Population Reaches 6.3 Million," 2000.

This data reveal a disturbing trend: A majority of those being released to parole will not successfully complete their terms, and the percentage of "unsuccessful" parolees is increasing. As Beck (1999) reported, annual discharges from state parole supervision reveal a sharp drop in the percent of parolees who successfully complete their term of community supervision. As a percentage of all discharges from state parole supervision, offenders successfully completing parole declined from 70 percent in 1984 to 42 percent in 1999 (Hughes, Wilson, and Beck, 2001). Note that the percentage of adults who successfully completed parole remained fairly steady after 1996, about 43 percent in 1999 (*see* Figure 2).

Parolees and Other "Conditional Releasees" Returned to Custody

Such high parole revocation rates are one of the major factors linked to the growing U.S. prison populations. Since 1980, the percentage of conditional release violators—who had originally left state prisons as parolees, mandatory releasees, and other type of releasees subject to community supervision—has more than doubled, from 16 percent to 33.8 percent (*see* Table 5).

TABLE 5: PERCENT OF ADMITTED PRISONERS, WHO WERE PAROLE VIOLATORS, SELECTED YEARS

State	1980	1985	1992	1997	1999
New York	24.1	13.8	13.9	23.0	30.0*
Pennsylvania	19.6	26.7	18.6	33.4	35.5
Ohio	18.5	21.1	16.6	19.6	17.3
Illinois	20.3	29.9	19.7	30.4	27.4
Michigan	16.6	23.5	25.8	28.3	34.6
North Carolina	10.6	5.8	17.4	23.6	5.1*
Georgia	8.2	18.3	25.5	23.0	18.2
Florida	16.0	6.4	12.7	12.2	6.9
Texas	15.8	30.9	39.9	22.7	30.0
California	20.7	41.7	56.3	64.7	66.1
Average:					
All fifty states	16.09	22.3	28.6	33.8	34.8
Federal only	11.09	12.9	/	9.0	/
State and federal combined	15.8	21.6	28.6	32.3	/

Note: "/" means not reported, or complete data not available; "*" means "violations only" reported for 1999 (not including violation and new felony).

Source: Bureau of Justice Statistics, *Correctional Populations in the United States*, 1980, 1985, 1992; unpublished data from 1997; Camp and Camp, 2000; Hughes, Wilson, and Beck, 2001.

In some states, the figures are even more dramatic. For example, in California, in 1999, more than two-thirds (67.2 percent) of all persons admitted to state prisons were parole violators. By comparison, in New York, the figure was just over 30 percent. In Texas, the state most comparable in prison population to California, the figure is just about 20 percent (Hughes, Wilson, and Beck, 2001). A report concluded: "There is no question that California has the highest rate of parole violations in the nation. In terms of total numbers, California accounts for nearly 40 percent of all known parole violators that occur in the nation although it reflects less than 15 percent of the nation's parole population" (Little Hoover Commission, 1998:23).

Contribution of Parolees to Crime

Another way to examine parole effectiveness is to look at the proportion of all persons arrested and in custody who were on "parole" at the time they committed their last crime. The Bureau of Justice Statistics conducts periodic surveys of persons arrested, in jail, in prison, and on death row. These data show that 44 percent of all state prisoners in 1991 had committed their latest crimes while out on probation or parole (*see* Figure 10, page 61).

What Works?

Such high recidivism rates have led to the common perception that community supervision fails to protect the public and that "nothing works." As DiIulio (1997:41) writes: "While formally under supervision in the community, these prison inmate violations included more than 13,000 murders, some 39,0000 robberies and tens of thousands of other crimes. More than a quarter of all felons charged with gun crimes in 1992 were out on probation or parole."

Of course, it is important to remember that more than 80 percent of all parolees are on caseloads where they are seen less than twice a month, and the dollars available to support their supervision and services are generally less than $1,500 per offender—when effective treatment programs are estimated to cost $12,000 to $15,000 per year, per client (Institute of Medicine, 1990). It is no wonder that recidivism rates are so high. In a sense, we get what we pay for, and as yet, we have never chosen to invest sufficiently in parole programs. Nevertheless, most view these data as showing that the parole system is neither helping offenders nor protecting the public, and that major reform is needed.

CHAPTER SEVEN

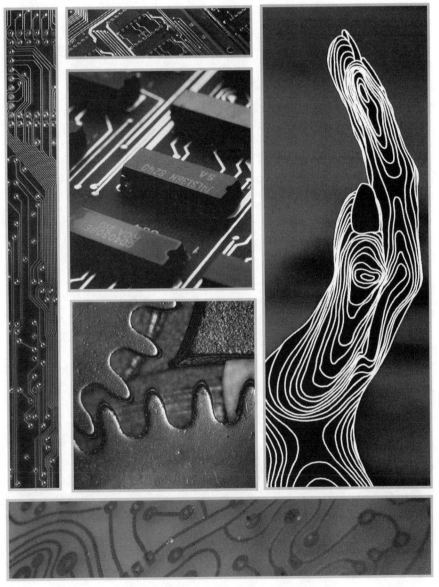

Parole Reform:
Reinventing and Reinvesting

As Joe Lehman, currently Commissioner of the Washington Department of Corrections, told the author:

> We have a broken parole system. Part of the problem is that parole can't do it alone, and we have misled the public in thinking that we can—hence the frustration, and the cries to abolish parole. We don't need to abolish parole, but a new model is sorely needed.

Interviews recently conducted with U.S. correctional experts reveal a consensus that parole needs to be "reinvented" (a term commonly used) and that the new parole "model" should incorporate at least four components:

1. Identifying dangerous and violent parolees, for whom surveillance through human and technological means is a top priority

2. Delivering quality treatment (particularly substance abuse) and job training programs to the subgroup of offenders for whom research shows such treatment could be most beneficial

3. Establishing intermediate sanctions and other means of diverting technical parole violators to community-based alternatives and away from expensive prison cells

4. Committing to a community-centered approach to parole supervision. This approach requires making a proactive commitment to managing offender risk in those neighborhoods where parolees live. It also means forming active partnerships with local police, community members, offenders' families, neighborhood associations, and other indigenous groups. Some refer to this as "neighborhood parole."

Greater Monitoring of High-risk, Violent Parolees

In 2000, ten states strengthened their interstate compact laws, and others granted officers of the parole court subpoena and house arrest authorities (National Conference of State Legislatures, 2001). No doubt the public, aided by private industry, will continue to demand and receive an increase in the level of control over certain violent, predatory offenders in the community.

Parolee Registration and the Internet

The most visible sign of this is the expanded registration of parolees, originally begun for sex offenders, but now expanding in terms of types of crimes and how accessible the information is to the public. Connecticut recently expanded its parolee registration to include kidnapping for sexual purposes, public indecency, and fourth-degree sexual assault. Florida's state website allows citizens to register to receive inmate release notifications.

A New York City-based crime victim's advocacy group, using information from the State Department of Correctional Services, now places on the Internet the names of inmates soon to be *eligible* for parole from New York State prisons in addition to including inmates' names, criminal background, and parole eligibility dates. The Internet site includes press clippings of the crime if they are available. The site encourages citizens to contact the New York State Division of Parole with comments. New Jersey citizens also can review and respond to parole candidates' profiles on their state's website.

In California, the State Department of Justice developed a CD-ROM database with the pictures, names, and whereabouts of the state's more than 50,000 registered sex offenders. Visitors to any local police station in the state are able to type in their ZIP codes and find out if a sex offender lives nearby. When the data was first released, many local newspapers published the pictures and addresses of local sex offenders. Los Angeles County announced in 1999 that, since few residents are using the CD-ROMs, they would begin mass mailings to residents informing them of the location and names of sex offenders living in their neighborhoods. Many states now maintain Internet sites with information about registered sex offenders; New Mexico, Colorado, Kentucky, Minnesota, and Rhode Island authorized new sites in 2000 (National Conference of State Legislatures, 2001).

New York and California both also now have 900-number hotlines set up to allow residents to check if someone is a registered sex offender. Before that, it was illegal for a law enforcement officer to notify citizens about a sex offender living in the neighborhood.

Other Technology for Community Monitoring of Parolees

Sophisticated technology is also assisting police and parole officers to keep better track of parolees once they return to the community. As the Cold War wound down, the defense industries, along with the developing computer and electronic industries, saw the community corrections clientele as a natural place to put its energies—a growing market. Electronic monitoring, voice verification systems, cheap on-site drug testing, breathalyzers through the phone—all allowed community corrections the option of becoming more surveillance-oriented.

Since the mid-1980s, the electronic monitoring industry has continued to expand, and three states (Texas, Florida, and New Jersey) now use global-positioning technology to determine when a parolee leaves his or her home or enters a restricted zone, such as an area around a school or the neighborhood of a former victim. The SMART (Satellite Monitoring and Remote Tracking) system was developed by Pro Tech Monitoring, Inc., a company founded by former Florida Governor Bob Martinez. "We integrated technologies proven in military and space applications to serve the citizens here at home," Martinez says. This new system helps criminal justice and law enforcement officials know where offenders are when the courts release them into our communities. The Florida Department of Corrections began implementing the system in 1997, and has transferred nearly 100 offenders from the old traditional house arrest systems to the SMART system (http://www.ptm.com/news.html). New Jersey began using the system in 1997 to monitor high-risk juveniles who have been mainly convicted of violent offenses or sexual assault. The technology also is being planned for counties in Minnesota and Pennsylvania (Kleinknecht, 1997). These initiatives and programs are a far cry from the traditional social work approaches to probation and parole.

Delivering Appropriate Treatment and Work Training to Selected Parolees

The public seems to have isolated its fear and punitiveness to the violent offender (in particular, the sexual offender), and seems more willing to tolerate treatment programs for nonviolent offenders, particularly substance abusers (Flanagan and Longmire, 1996). Recent research reveals that the public favors both punishing and treating criminals. Their punitiveness tends to be reduced when they are provided with complex sentencing options and informed about the high cost of incarceration (Applegate et al., 1996).

A recent study found the public unwilling to tolerate regular probation for felons, but willing to tolerate, if not prefer, strict community-based alternatives to prison when these sanctions are developed and applied meaningfully. For the crime of robbery with injury, for example, 50 percent of the respondents viewed a sanction between a halfway house and strict probation as acceptable. When the option of shock incarceration (prison followed by community supervision) is added, this figure rises to a full 63 percent (Sundt et al., 1998). The public seems open to tough community-based sanctions and wants them to include both treatment and surveillance.

This softening of public attitudes seems to have resulted from knowledge about the high costs of prisons, combined with emerging evidence that some treatment programs are effective, for some offenders, under certain empirically established conditions. This research has identified those principles that produce effective correctional interventions. The evidence indicates that well-designed and properly implemented programs incorporating these principles result in significant reductions in recidivism. Those programs that are most successful include a strong behavior and cognitive skills development component (Andrews and Bonta, 1994). Some of these programs have been effective in reducing the rearrest rates of parolees.

Drug and Alcohol Dependency Programs

A recent research summary of drug treatment effectiveness reported that "a growing body of research" shows that voluntary or mandatory drug treatment can reduce recidivism, especially when treatment is matched to offender needs (Prendergast, Anglin, and Wellisch, 1995). The most successful programs are based on social learning theory. These programs assume that criminal behavior is learned, so they try to improve offenders' interpersonal relations through vocational and social skill building, peer-oriented behavior programs, role playing, and interpersonal cognitive skill training. Effective treatment programs must also continue assisting the offender for several months after program completion (*see also* Latessa, 1999).

A program that attempts to do this with noted success is San Diego's Parolee Partnership Program (PPP), which is part of California's statewide Preventing Paroling Failure Program. The San Diego program, begun in 1992, provides substance abuse treatment for parolees in San Diego County. A private vendor operates the program, using principles of client selection, managed care, case management, and case follow-up. The vendor subcontracts to provide outpatient, residential and detoxification treatment services and facilities. Support services (for example, education, vocational training, and transportation) are provided directly by the vendor or through referral to other community resource agencies. Typically, the time limit is 180 days of treatment. The participant is then assigned a "recovery advocate" who motivates the offender to continue in treatment for as long as necessary and keeps the parole agent aware of the parolee's progress. The program served about 700 offenders in FY 1995-96 at a total cost of about $1.5 million (about $2,100 per parolee).

An evaluation of the program shows that the Parolee Partnership Program was successful with its target group (which was characterized as a hard-to-treat group, who on average had used drugs for about eleven years). The percentage of parolees placed in the program who were returned to prison was nearly 8 percentage points lower than the return rate for the statistically matched comparison group, and this difference was statistically significant (California Department of Corrections, 1997). Los Angeles County operates a similarly successful program.

The success of these programs motivated the California State Legislature to increase funding for parole substance abuse programs in 1998-2000.

Employment and Job Training

Research consistently has shown that if parolees can find decent jobs as soon as possible after release, they are less likely to return to crime and to prison. Several parole programs have been successful at securing employment for parolees.

The Texas RIO (Re-Integration of Offenders) Project, begun as a two-city pilot program in 1985, has become one of the nation's most ambitious government programs devoted to placing parolees in jobs (Finn, 1998c). RIO has more than 100 staff members in 62 offices who provide job placement services to nearly 16,000 parolees each year in every county in Texas (or nearly half of all parolees released from Texas prisons each year). RIO claims to have placed 75 percent of more than 200,000 ex-offenders since 1985.

RIO represents a collaboration of two state agencies, the Texas Workforce Commission, where the program is housed, and the Texas Department of Criminal Justice, whose RIO-funded assessment specialists help inmates prepare for employment and whose parole officers refer released inmates to the program. As the reputation of the program has spread, the Texas Workforce Commission has developed a pool of more than 12,000 employers who have hired parolees referred by the RIO program.

A 1992 independent evaluation documented that 60 percent of the RIO participants found employment, compared with 36 percent of a matched group of non-RIO parolees. In addition, one year after release, RIO participants had worked at some time during three-month intervals more than had comparison group members. During the year after release, when most recidivism occurs, 48 percent of the RIO high-risk clients were rearrested compared with 57 percent of the non-RIO high-risk parolees; only 23 percent of the high-risk RIO participants returned to prison, compared with 38 percent of a comparable group of non-RIO parolees (Finn, 1998c). In fiscal year 1997, approximately 77 percent of Texas' ex-offenders found employment; the Texas Workforce Commission predicted that

66 percent of those employed would not return to prison (Fulp, 2001). The evaluation also concluded that the program continually saved the state money—more than $5 million in 1990 alone—by helping to reduce the number of parolees who otherwise would have been rearrested and sent back to prison (Fulp, 2001). These positive findings encouraged the Texas legislature to increase RIO's annual budget to more than $3 million, and other states (for example, Georgia) have implemented aspects of the RIO model.

New York City's Center for Employment Opportunities (CEO) project is a transitional service for parolees, consisting of day labor work crews. Assignment to a work crew begins immediately after release from prison, and while it is designed to prepare inmates for placement in a permanent job, it also helps to provide structure, instill work habits, and earn early daily income (Finn, 1998b). Most participants are young offenders, released from prison boot camp programs, and they are required to enroll as a condition of parole. The descriptive evaluation of this program shows that young parolees associated with the program are more likely to be employed, refrain from substance use, and participate in community service and education while in the Center for Employment Opportunities program.

Multiservice Centers

The Safer Foundation, headquartered in Chicago, is now the largest community-based provider of employment services for ex-offenders in the United States, with a professional staff of nearly 200 in 6 locations in 2 states. The Safer Foundation offers a wide range of services for parolees, including employment, education, and housing. A 1998 evaluation shows that Safer has helped more than 40,000 participants find jobs since 1972, and nearly two-thirds of those placed kept their jobs for thirty days or more of continuous employment (Finn, 1998a). Since the summer of 1997, Safer reports finding jobs for more than 3,000 ex-offenders, 73 percent of whom retained their jobs after 30 days (Tonn, 2001). Safer's Youth Empowerment Program, designed for juvenile probation and parole education, enjoys comparable success. Approximately 80 percent complete training (the vast majority of whom are placed in jobs or vocational training), and participants are 53 percent less likely than nonparticipants to be convicted of a new crime in Illinois (Tonn, 1999).

Another highly successful program for released prisoners is operated by Pioneer Human Services in Seattle, Washington, a private, nonprofit organization. Pioneer Human Services provides housing, jobs, and social support for released offenders, but it also operates sheltered workshops for the hard-to-place offender. It is different from other social-service agencies in that its program is funded almost entirely by the profits from the various businesses it operates, and not through grants. They place a priority on practical living skills and job training. Most of their clients are able to maintain employment either in the free market or for Pioneer Human Services, and the recidivism rate is less than 5 percent for its work-release participants (Turner and Petersilia, 1996b).

Benefits of Quality Treatment and Programs

There are parole programs that work. One of the immediate challenges is to find the money to pay for them. Martin Horn, former secretary of the Pennsylvania Department of Corrections, suggests using offender "vouchers" to pay for parole programs. At the end of the prisoner's term, the offender would be provided with vouchers with which he or she could purchase certain types of services upon release (for example drug and alcohol treatment, job placement, and family counseling). Mr. Horn suggests giving $2,000 in "service coupons" for each of the two years following prison release. Offenders then could purchase the services they feel they most need. Mr. Horn's cost-benefit analysis for this plan for the state of Pennsylvania shows that it could save the state about $50 million per year—dollars that he says then could be invested in prevention programs instead of prison (Horn, 2001).

Intermediate Sanctions for Parole Violators

States are taking a new look at how they respond to violations of parole—particularly technical violations that do not involve new criminal behavior (Burke, 1997). Several states are now structuring their courts' responses to technical violations. Missouri opened up the Kansas City Recycling Center in 1988, a forty-one-bed facility operated by a private contractor to deal exclusively with technical violators who have been recommended for revocation. The pilot program proved so successful that the state took over operation and set aside a complete correctional facility of 250 beds for the program. Mississippi and Georgia use ninety-day boot camp programs, housed in separate wings of the state prisons, for probation violators (for other program descriptions, *see* Parent et al., 1994). While empirical evidence as to the effects of these programs is scant, system officials believe that the programs serve to increase the certainty of punishment, while reserving scarce prison space for the truly violent. Importantly, experts (*see* Travis, Solomon, and Waul, 2001) believe that states with "intermediate" (nonprison) options for responding to less serious parole violations are able to reduce parolees' new commitments to prison, explaining the vast differences shown in Table 5 on page 171.

"Neighborhood" Parole

One of the critical lessons learned during the past decade has been that no one program—surveillance or rehabilitation alone—or any one agency—police without parole, parole without mental health, or any of these agencies outside the community—can reduce crime, or fear of crime, on its own (Petersilia, 1998a). Crime and criminality are complex, multifaceted problems, and real long-term solutions must come from the community, and be actively participated in by the community, and those that surround the offender. This model of community engagement is the foundation of community policing, and its tenants are now spreading to probation and parole.

This new parole model is being referred to as "neighborhood parole" (Smith and Dickey, 1998), "corrections of place" (Clear and Corbett, 1999), or "police-parole partnerships" (Morgan and Marrs, 1998). Regardless of the name, the key components are the same. They involve: strengthening parole's linkages with law enforcement and the community; offering a "full-service" model of parole; and attempting to change the offenders' lives through personal, family, and neighborhood interventions. At the core, these models move away from managing parolees on conventional caseloads, and towards a more "activist supervision," where agents are responsible for close supervision and procuring jobs, social support, and needed treatment.

The "neighborhood parole" model has been most well thought out in Wisconsin, where the Governor's Task Force on Sentencing and Corrections recommended the program. Program proponents realize neighborhood-based parole will be more costly than traditional parole supervision, but they are hopeful that reduced recidivism and revocations to prison will offset program costs. In 1998, the Wisconsin legislature allocated $8 million to fund and evaluate the Dane and Racine counties' pilot Enhanced Supervision Projects (Smith and Dickey, 1998). The programs were so successful, State Senator Gwendolyne Moore requested then-Governor Tommy G. Thompson to allocate further money and position authority in their 2001-2003 budget to replicate the programs in Milwaukee, Rock, and Menominee counties (Moore, 2000).

CHAPTER EIGHT

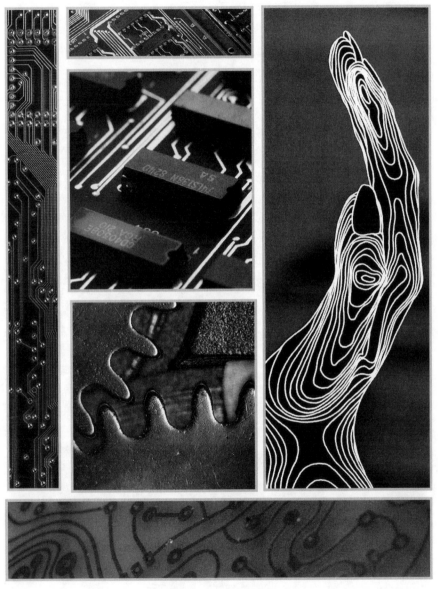

Conclusion

Nearly 700,000 parolees are now doing their time on U.S. streets. Most have been released to parole systems that provide few services and impose conditions that almost guarantee their failure. Our monitoring systems are getting better, and public tolerance for failure on parole is decreasing. The result is that a rising tide of parolees is washing back into prison, putting pressure on states to build more prisons, which in turn, takes money away from rehabilitation programs that might have helped offenders while they were in the community. All of this means that parolees will continue to receive fewer services to help them deal with their underlying problems, assuring that recidivism rates and returns to prison remain high—and public support for parole remain low.

This situation represents a formidable challenge to those concerned with crime and punishment. The public will not support community-based punishments until they have been shown to "work," and they will not have an opportunity to "work" without sufficient funding and research. Spending on parole services in California, for example, was cut 44 percent in 1997, causing parole caseloads to nearly double (to a ratio of eighty-two to one). When caseloads increase, services decline, and even parolees who are motivated to change have little opportunity to do so. Job training programs are cut, and parolees often remain at the end of long waiting lists for community-based drug and alcohol treatment.

Yet, crime committed by parolees is a real problem, and there is every reason to be skeptical about our ability to reduce it significantly. Early parole research did not reveal any easy fixes, and the current parole population is increasingly difficult and dangerous. The public is skeptical that the "experts" know how to solve the crime problem, and increasingly have taken matters into their own hands. Corrections officials report being increasingly constrained by political forces, and no longer being allowed to use their own best judgments on crime policy (Rubin, 1997). State officials feel that even a single visible failure of any parole program readily could become a political disaster for the existing administration. One notorious case was that of Willie Horton and the Massachusetts furlough program. The press often publicizes such cases to feed the public's appetite for news about the failure of the criminal justice system. Such negative news, and the fear of such negative news, often precludes any innovative parole reform efforts.

The challenge is to bring greater balance to the handling of parole populations by singling out those offenders who represent different public safety risks and different prospects for rehabilitation. The pilot parole programs described in the previous chapter are the first step, but it would help considerably if rigorous impact evaluations were always conducted. We do not know with any precision what impact parole has on offenders' recidivism, or what supervision conditions are helpful to the reintegration process.

It is safe to say that parole programs have received less research attention than any other correctional component in recent years. A congressionally mandated evaluation of state and local crime prevention programs included just one parole evaluation among the hundreds of recent studies that were summarized for that effort (Sherman et al., 1997). The author of this essay has spent many years contributing to the evaluation literature on *probation* effectiveness but knows of no similar body of knowledge on *parole* effectiveness. Without better information, it is unlikely that the public will give corrections officials the political permission to invest in rehabilitation and job training programs for parolees. With better information, we might be able to persuade the voters and elected officials to shift their current preferences away from solely punitive crime policies, and toward a sanctioning philosophy that balances incapacitation, rehabilitation, and just punishment.

The United States now has more than two million people in jails and prisons, and more people on parole than ever before. If current parole revocation trends continue, more than half of all those entering prison each year will be parole failures. Given the increasing human and financial costs associated with prison, investing in effective reentry programs may well be one of the best investments we make.

QUESTIONS AND ANSWERS

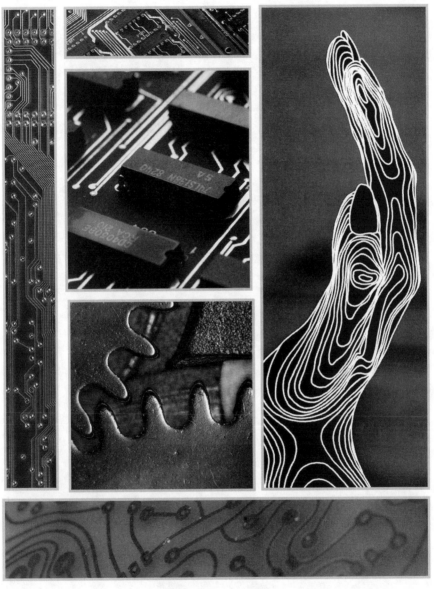

Parole and Prisoner Reentry in the United States

Multiple Choice Questions:

Circle the letter of the correct answer.

1. Most U.S. prisoners are released from prison on:
   a. Work furlough
   b. Shock probation
   c. Boot camp
   d. Parole

2. The term "parole" refers to:
   a. Both a release mechanism and a method of community supervision
   b. Community supervision
   c. Postprison treatment programs
   d. A method of releasing persons from prison

3. The Bureau of Justice Statistics (BJS) reports what rearrest rate of parolees?
   a. 25 percent within three years
   b. 40 percent within three years
   c. 62 percent within three years
   d. 99 percent within three years

4. The use of determinate sentencing and parole guidelines to fix the end of a prisoner's incarceration is referred to as:
   a. Mandatory release
   b. Guided discretion
   c. Parole professionalism
   d. Judicial parole

5. *Morrissey v. Brewer* (1972) is a landmark case most directly related to which subject?
   a. Parole revocation
   b. Appointment of parole board members
   c. Compensation to crime victims for injuries caused by parolees
   d. Denial of parole

6. The authority of the parole board is called:
   a. Exemplary sanction
   b. Discretionary release
   c. Administrative direction
   d. Pardon

7. According to Petersilia, what is the main reason that services are not currently delivered to most parolees?
   a. Parole supervision has been transformed to a law enforcement system
   b. Parolees do not want any services
   c. All available services are given to probationers
   d. Crime victims advocate against services for the parolees

8. Recent national recidivism data reveal:
   a. Fewer parolees are failing supervision
   b. More parolees are failing supervision
   c. Only sex offenders have high failure rates
   d. Only unemployed offenders have high failure rates

9. Legal restrictions that prevent released felons from voting and holding elective office, engaging in certain professions and occupations, and associating with known offenders are known as:
   a. Civil disabilities
   b. Crime restrictions
   c. Technical violations
   d. Technical restrictions

10. Which of the following is not a component of "reinvented" parole?
    a. Diverting technical violators to community-based alternatives
    b. Prioritizing dangerous and violent parolees for highest surveillance
    c. Committing to a community-centered approach to parole supervision
    d. Eliminating substance abuse treatment programs

11. Which of the following is a function of a parole board?
    a. Release inmates into the community prior to expiration of sentence
    b. Set policies governing community supervision
    c. Revoke parolee liberty and return parolee to prison
    d. All of the above

12. Which state leads the nation in terms of the percentage of parolees who are returned to prison?
    a. Texas
    b. Massachusetts
    c. California
    d. Florida

13. How are parole guidelines defined?
    a. Actuarial devices which predict the risk of recidivism based on crime and offender information
    b. Legal opinions regarding the parole revocation process
    c. Manuals identifying successful parole programs
    d. None of the above

14. Most parolees are supervised on _____ caseloads.
    a. Regular
    b. Intensive
    c. Electronic
    d. Specialized

15. How are members of most United States parole boards selected?
    a. Political appointees
    b. A civil service exam
    c. Appointed by the U.S. President
    d. Appointed by the Director of Corrections

16. Which two states do not have parole supervision requirements?
    a. Georgia and Alabama
    b. Virginia and Tennessee
    c. Maine and Virginia
    d. Michigan and Illinois

17. What are the ways in which parole is revoked?
    a. Technical violation or new crime
    b. New crime or restraining order
    c. Restraining order or writ of habeas corpus
    d. Writ of habeas corpus or technical violation

18. Violations of the conditions of parole are referred to as:
    a. Mandatory violations
    b. Technical violations
    c. Serious violations
    d. New crime violations

19. As of 2001, how many states had abolished discretionary parole?
    a. 2
    b. 7
    c. 14
    d. 35

20. Legislatures concerned with the correctional goal of treatment will prescribe:
    a. Mandatory sentencing
    b. Indeterminate sentencing
    c. Definite sentencing
    d. Determinate sentencing

21. The required release of inmates at the expiration of a certain time period is called:
    a. Discretionary release
    b. Mandatory release
    c. Conditional release
    d. Provisional release

22. The major conclusion of Robert Martinson's study of correctional program effectiveness concluded:
    a. Rehabilitation programs have no appreciable effect on recidivism
    b. Job training programs reduce recidivism
    c. Treatment programs only help those offenders who volunteer
    d. Rehabilitation programs reduce recidivism

23. The most common method for state prisoners to be released today is:
    a. Discretionary parole
    b. Mandatory release
    c. Expiration releases
    d. Pardon

24. Parole officers are authorized to carry weapons:
    a. In two-thirds of the states
    b. In California only
    c. In Texas only
    d. Nowhere in the United States

25. Parole comes from the French word parol, meaning:
    a. "Word," as in giving one's word of honor
    b. "Word," as in promising to make victim restitution
    c. "Ticket of leave," as in early release
    d. "Ticket of leave," as in to relieve prison crowding

Short Essay Questions:

Answer the following in complete sentences

1. Why is parole frequently criticized, and which groups have argued for its abolition?
2. Discuss the changing nature of parole supervision and services.
3. What are the most common standard parole conditions imposed throughout the United States?
4. In most states, convicted felons (including sex offenders) lose certain rights as citizens and employees. Discuss some of the pros and cons of these and other "civil disabilities."
5. According to the author, what impact do parole violators have on the size and composition of the prison population? What are some programs to address these issues?

Multiple Choice Answers:

1.	d.	14.	a.
2.	a.	15.	a.
3.	c.	16.	c.
4.	a.	17.	a.
5.	a.	18.	b.
6.	b.	19.	c.
7.	a.	20.	b.
8.	b.	21.	b.
9.	a.	22.	a.
10.	d.	23.	b.
11.	d.	24.	a.
12.	c.	25.	a.
13.	a.		

Short Essay Answers:

1. **Why is parole frequently criticized, and which groups have argued for its abolition?**

Parole has never received much public support. In the 1970s, it seemed as if everyone felt it needed major revamping. Citizen groups claimed that it unfairly reduced prison sentences imposed on serious offenders. When offenders were "let out early," as citizens often perceived discretionary parole release, they said it trivialized the seriousness of offenders' crimes and diminished the damage done to victims. Academics said that parole boards were unable to predict which inmates would return to crime after release, and hence the discretionary release decision was fraught with personal biases and prejudices, with little empirical justification. Politicians argued that the system lacked transparency and credibility, as neither victims nor offenders knew exactly how much prison time would be served. They also argued that discretionary parole release diminished the deterrent aspects of sentencing, since the length of the prison term was unknown at sentencing. Media attacks upon parole have centered on recidivism, and have highlighted the so-called revolving door of prisons to represent the failure of parole. Finally, prisoners argued that not knowing their release date put additional psychological pressures on them, since they could not plan for release and they had to play games with the parole board to "look good" for them. All believed that rehabilitation programs were wasted on inmates who were simply participating in them to obtain release, rather than to benefit truly from services.

2. **Discuss the changing nature of parole supervision and services.**

Historically, parole agents were viewed as paternalistic figures that mixed authority with help. Officers provided direct services (such as counseling) and also knew the community and brokered services (such as job training) to needy offenders. Parole was originally designed to make the transition from prison to the community more gradual and, during this time, parole officers were to assist the offender in addressing personal problems and searching for employment and a place to live. Many parole agencies still do assist in these "service" activities. Increasingly, however, parole supervision has shifted away from providing services to parolees, and more toward monitoring and surveillance activities (such as drug testing, monitoring curfews, and collecting restitution).

There are a number of reasons for this shift. For one, a greater number of parole conditions are being assigned to released prisoners. Parolees in state systems are more frequently being required to submit to drug testing, complete community service, and make restitution payments. Parole officers work for the corrections system, and if paroling authorities are imposing a greater number of conditions on parolees, then field agents must monitor those conditions. As a result, modern day parole officers have less time to provide other services, such as counseling, even if they were inclined to do so.

It is also true that the fiscal crisis experienced in most states has reduced the number of treatment and job training programs in the community-at-large, and given the fear and suspicion surrounding ex-convicts, these persons are usually placed at the end of the waiting lists. The ability to "broker" services to parolees, given the scarcity of programs, has become increasingly difficult.

The main reason, however, that "services" are not delivered to most parolees is that parole supervision has been transformed ideologically from a social service to a law enforcement system. Just as the prison system responded to the public's demands for accountability and justice, so did parole officers.

3. **What are the most common standard parole conditions imposed throughout the United States?**

Standard conditions are similar throughout most jurisdictions, and violating them can result in a return to prison. Common standard parole conditions include the following:

- Report to the parole agent within twenty-four hours of release
- Do not carry weapons
- Report changes of address and employment
- Do not travel more than fifty miles from home or leave the county for more than forty-eight hours without prior approval from the parole agent
- Obey all parole agent instructions
- Seek and maintain employment, or participate in education/work training
- Do not commit crimes
- Submit to search by the police and parole officers

4. **In most states, convicted felons (including sex offenders) lose certain rights as citizens and employees. Discuss some of the pros and cons of these and other "civil disabilities."**

In many ways, prisoners leave prison with only part of their debt to society paid. Much more is owed, and may never be paid off. For example, one of the traditional consequences of a felony conviction has been the loss of voting rights. The laws of forty-six states and the District of Columbia contain such stipulations. Fourteen states permanently deny convicted felons the right to vote. Eighteen states suspend the right to vote until the offender has completed the sentence and paid all fines. As a result, some 4 million Americans, 1.4 million of whom are African-American (equaling 13 percent of the black male adult population), are disenfranchised by this.

With a spate of laws beginning in the late 1980s, a number of states now require that sex offenders be registered with the police upon release from prison, and/or that the community be notified that a sex offender is living in their neighborhood. Today, every state requires convicted sex offenders to register with law enforcement on release (so called "Megan's Laws").

Public employment is also permanently denied in six states: Alabama, Delaware, Iowa, Mississippi, Rhode Island, and South Carolina. The remaining jurisdictions permit public employment in varying degrees. Since public employment is a major source of jobs for unskilled laborers, these restrictions severely limit the job opportunities available to ex-convicts.

These kinds of disqualifications and burdens constitute a very real component of the punishment. Taken together, they reflect a philosophy where ex-offenders are cut off from civic participation, banned from certain employment opportunities, and required to display their status as an ex-offender, when required. Such restrictions lead to greater alienation and disillusionment with the political process and erode residents' feelings of commitment and makes them less willing to participate in local activities. This is important, since our most effective crime fighting tools require community collaboration and active engagement.

5. According to the author, what impact do parole violators have on the size and composition of the prison population? What are some programs to address these issues?

Nearly 700,000 parolees are now doing their time on United States streets. Our monitoring systems are getting more sophisticated, and a greater number of parolees are failing parole supervision. The result is that a rising tide of parolees is washing back into prison, putting pressure on states to build more prisons, which in turn, takes money away from rehabilitation programs that might have helped offenders while they were in the community.

This rise in rates of parole failures, on an increasing base of parole populations, has had a profound impact on the nation's prison population. In 1980, parole violators constituted 18 percent of prison admissions; they now constitute 37 percent of prisoners coming in the "front door." In 1998, this meant that 207,000 of the 565,000 people admitted to prison were parole violators, individuals who had either been returned to prison on a "technical violation" or for committing a new offense. The combination of this increase, with the leveling off of new prison commitments from new convictions, means that parole revocations are now a significant factor in the rising prison populations.

States are taking a new look at how they respond to violations of parole—particularly technical violations that do not involve, of themselves, new criminal behavior. Several states are now structuring the court's responses to technical violations. Missouri operates a forty-one-bed facility to deal exclusively with technical violators who have been recommended for revocation. Other states use various intermediate sanction programs to divert parolees from prison. While empirical evidence as to the effects of these programs is scant, system officials believe that the programs serve to increase the certainty of punishment, while reserving scarce prison space for the truly violent.

PART II REFERENCES

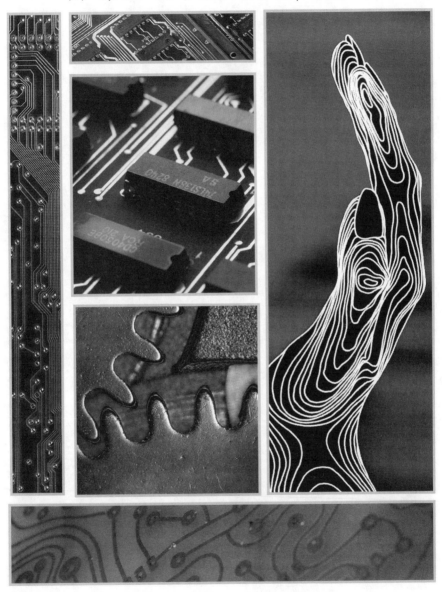

Abadinsky, Howard. 1997. *Probation and Parole.* Upper Saddle River, New Jersey: Simon and Schuster.

Adams, William, and Jeffrey Roth. 1998. "Federal Offenders under Community Supervision, 1987-96." Washington, D.C.: Bureau of Justice Statistics.

Allard, Patricia, and Marc Mauer. 2000. "Regaining the Vote: An Assessment of Activity Relating to Felon Disenfranchisement Laws." Washington, D.C.: The Sentencing Project.

Allen, George. 1997. "Abolishing Parole Saves Lives and Property." *Corrections Today.* 59(4):22.

American Correctional Association. 2000. *Vital Statistics in Corrections.* Lanham, Maryland: American Correctional Association.

————. 1998. *Probation and Parole Directory.* Lanham, Maryland: American Correctional Association.

————. 2001a. "Parole." *Corrections Compendium.* 26 (6):8-22.

————. 2001b. *Probation and Parole Directory.* Lanham, Maryland: American Correctional Association.

Andrews, Don and James Bonta. 1994. *The Psychology of Criminal Conduct.* Cincinnati, Ohio: Anderson Publishing.

Applegate, Brian, Frances Cullen, Michael Turner, and Jody Sundt. 1996. "Assessing Public Support for Three-Strikes-You're Out Laws: Global Versus Specific Attitudes." *Crime and Delinquency.* 42:517-534.

Association of Paroling Authorities, International. 2000. "Parole Board Survey 1999." Washington, D.C.: Association of Paroling Authorities, International.

Austin, James, Charles Jones, John Kramer, and Phil Renninger. 1996. "National Assessment of Structured Sentencing." Washington, D.C.: U.S. Department of Justice, Bureau of Justice Assistance.

Austin, James, and Robert Lawson. 1998. "Assessment of California Parole Violations and Recommended Intermediate Programs and Policies." San Francisco: National Council on Crime and Delinquency.

Beck, Allen J. 1999. "Trends in U.S. Correctional Populations." In Kenneth Haas and Geoffrey Alpert, eds. *The Dilemmas of Corrections.* Prospect Heights, Illinois: Waveland Press, Inc. 44-100.

————. 2000. "Prisoners in 1999." Washington, D.C.: U.S. Department of Justice, Bureau of Justice Statistics.

Beck, Allen, and Bernard Shipley. 1989. "Recidivism of Prisoners Released in 1983." Washington D.C.: U.S. Department of Justice, Bureau of Justice Statistics.

Bottomly, Keith A. 1990. "Parole in Transition: A Comparative Study of Origins, Developments, and Prospects for the 1990s." In Michael Tonry and Norval Morris, eds. *Crime and Justice: A Review of Research.* Chicago: University of Chicago Press. 319-374.

Bureau of Justice Statistics. 1977-1997. "National Prisoner Statistics." Washington, D.C.: U.S. Department of Justice, Bureau of Justice Statistics.

————. 1980, 1985, 1992. *Correctional Populations in the United States.* Washington, D.C.: U.S. Department of Justice, Bureau of Justice Statistics.

————. 1981, 1986-1997. *Annual Parole Survey.* Washington, D.C.: U.S. Department of Justice, Bureau of Justice Statistics.

————. 1985, 1990, 1996. *National Corrections Reporting Program.* Washington, D.C.: U.S. Department of Justice, Bureau of Justice Statistics.

————. 1997. "National Corrections Reporting Program 1996." Washington, D.C.: U.S. Department of Justice, Bureau of Justice Statistics.

————. 1998. "Probation and Parole Populations 1997." Washington, D.C.: U.S. Department of Justice, Bureau of Justice Statistics.

————. 2000. "U.S. Correctional Population Reaches 6.3 Million Men and Women: Represents 3.1 Percent of the Adult U.S. Population." Washington, D.C.: U.S. Department of Justice, Bureau of Justice Statistics.

————. 2001a. "Federal Criminal Case Processing, 1999." Washington, D.C.: U.S. Department of Justice, Bureau of Justice Statistics.

————. 2001b. "Probation and Parole in the United States, 2000." Washington, D.C.: U.S. Department of Justice, Bureau of Justice Statistics.

Burke, Peggy B. 1995. "Abolishing Parole: Why the Emperor Has No Clothes." Lexington, Kentucky: American Probation and Parole Association.

————. 1997. "Policy-Driven Responses to Probation and Parole Violations." Washington, D.C.: National Institute of Corrections.

Butterfield, Fox. 1999. "Eliminating Parole Boards Isn't a Cure-All, Experts Say." *New York Times*. January 10:11.

California Department of Corrections. 1997. "Preventing Parolee Failure Program: An Evaluation." Sacramento: California Department of Corrections.

————. 2001. "CDC Facts" Sacramento. http://www.cdc.state.ca.us/factsht.htm.

Camp, Camille and George Camp. 1999. *The Corrections Yearbook*. Middletown, Connecticut: Criminal Justice Institute, Inc.

————. 2000. *The Corrections Yearbook*. Middletown, Connecticut: Criminal Justice Institute, Inc.

Carter, Beth. 1998. "Harbingers of Change." Crime and Politics in the 1990s: Creating Demand for New Policies. Conference materials at Campaign for an Effective Crime Policy, February 15-17, Washington, D.C.

Citizens' Inquiry on Parole and Criminal Justice. 1974. "Report on New York Parole." New York City, New York: The Citizen's Inquiry.

Clear, Todd and George Cole. 1997. *American Corrections*. Belmont, California.: Wadsworth Publishing.

Clear, Todd and Ronald Corbett. 1999. "Community Corrections of Place." *Perspectives*. 23:24-32.

Corrections Digest. 2000. "Reno Praises Boston Re-Entry Court Pilot." *Corrections Digest*. 12, January.

Cromwell, Paul F. and Rolando del Carmen. 1999. *Community Based Corrections*. Belmont, California: West/Wadsworth.

del Carmen, Rolando and James Alan Pilant. 1994. "The Scope of Judicial Immunity for Probation and Parole Officers." *APPA Perspectives*. 18:14-21.

Deschenes, Elizabeth, Susan Turner, and Joan Petersilia. 1995. "A Dual Experiment in Intensive Community Supervision: Minnesota's Prison Diversion and Enhanced Supervised Released Programs." *The Prison Journal*. 75.

DiIulio, John. 1997. "Reinventing Parole and Probation." *The Brookings Review*. 40, 42.

Ditton, Paula and Doris James Wilson. 1999. "Truth in Sentencing in State Prisons." Washington, D.C.: Bureau of Justice Statistics.

Fabelo, Tony. 1999. "Biennial Report to the 76th Texas Legislature." Austin, Texas: Criminal Justice Policy Council.

Fagan, Jeffrey. 1998. "Treatment and Reintegration of Violent Offenders." In B. J. Auerbach and T. C. Castellano, eds. *Successful Community Sanctions and Services for Special Offenders: Proceedings of the 1994 Conference of the International Community Corrections Association*. Lanham, Maryland: American Correctional Association and the International Community Corrections Association.

Feeley, Malcolm and Jonathan Simon. 1992. "The New Penology: Notes on the Emerging Strategy of Corrections and its Implications." *Criminology*. 30:449-474.

Finn, Peter. 1998a. "Chicago's Safer Foundation: A Road Back for Ex-Offenders." Washington, D.C.: National Institute of Justice.

———. 1998b. "Successful Job Placement for Ex-Offenders: The Center for Employment Opportunities." Washington, D.C.: National Institute of Justice.

———. 1998c. "Texas' Project RIO (Re-Integration of Offenders)." Washington, D.C.: National Institute of Justice.

Flanagan, Timothy. 1996. "Reform or Punish: Americans' Views of the Correctional System." In Timothy Flanagan and Dennis Longmire, eds. *Americans View Crime and Justice*. Thousand Oaks, California: Sage Publications.

Flanagan, Timothy and Dennis Longmire, eds. 1996. *Americans View Crime and Justice: A National Public Opinion Survey*. Thousand Oaks, California: Sage Publications.

Fogel, David. 1975. *We Are the Living Proof*. Cincinnati, Ohio: Anderson.

Freeman, Robert M. 2000. *Popular Culture and Corrections*. Lanham, Maryland: American Correctional Association.

Fulp, Elmer. 2001. "Project RIO: Reintegration of Offenders." In *The State of Corrections: Proceedings, American Correctional Association, Annual Conferences, 2000.* Lanham, Maryland: American Correctional Association.

Gainsborough, Jenni. 1997. "Eliminating Parole is a Dangerous and Expensive Proposition." *Corrections Today.* 59(4):23.

The Gallup Organization. 1998. "Gallup Surveys Pertaining to Parole (special request)." New York, New York: The Gallup Organization.

Glaser, Daniel. 1969. *The Effectiveness of a Prison and Parole System.* Indianapolis, Indiana: Bobbs-Merrill.

Golde v. Fox, 98 Cal. App. 3d 167, 159 *California Reporter* 864, 1st District 1979.

Gottfredson, Don, Peter Hoffman, and M. Sigler. 1975. "Making Parole Policy Explicit." *Crime and Delinquency.* January:7-17.

Gottfredson, Don, Leslie Wilkins, and Peter Hoffman. 1978. *Guidelines for Parole and Sentencing.* Lexington, Massachusetts: Heath/Lexington.

Hinton, Mick. 2001. "Pace of Processing Keeping Parolees on Prisons' Budget." *The Oklahoman.* March 1.

Hoffman, Peter B. and Lucille K. DeGostin. 1974. "Parole Decision Making: Structuring Discretion." *Federal Probation.* December.

Holt, Norman. 1998. "The Current State of Parole in America." In Joan Petersilia, ed. *Community Corrections: Probation, Parole, and Intermediate Sanctions.* New York: Oxford University Press. 28-41.

Horn, Martin F. 2001. "Rethinking Sentencing." *Corrections Management Quarterly.* 5(3).

Hughes, Timothy A., Doris James Wilson, and Allen J. Beck. 2001. "Trends in State Parole, 1990-2000." Washington, D.C.: U.S. Department of Justice, Bureau of Justice Statistics.

Institute of Medicine. 1990. D. R. Gerstein and H. J. Harwood, eds. *Treating Drug Problems: A Study of the Evolution, Effectiveness, and Financing of Public and Private Drug Treatment Systems.* Washington, D.C.: National Academy Press.

Irwin, John and James Austin. 1994. *It's About Time: America's Imprisonment Binge.* Belmont, California: Wadsworth Publishing Company.

Kleinknecht, William. 1997. "Juvenile Authorities Want Satellite Tracking for Felons." *The Star-Ledger* (New Jersey). November 18:7.

Latessa, Edward, ed. 1999. *Strategic Solutions: The International Community Corrections Association Examines Substance Abuse.* Lanham, Maryland: American Correctional Association and the International Community Corrections Association.

Legislative Analysts Office. 1998. "Reforming California's Adult Parole System." Sacramento: Legislative Analysts Office.

Lieb, Roxanne, Vernon Quinsey, and Lucy Berliner. 1998. "Sexual Predators and Social Policy." In Michael Tonry, ed. *Crime and Justice: A Review of Research.* Chicago: University of Chicago Press.

Lipton, Douglas, Robert Martinson, and Judith Wilks. 1975. *The Effectiveness of Correctional Treatment and What Works: A Survey of Treatment Evaluation Studies.* New York: Praeger.

Little Hoover Commission. 1998. "Beyond Bars: Correctional Reforms to Lower Prison Costs and Reduce Crime." Sacramento, California: Little Hoover Commission.

Love, Margaret and Susan Kuzma. 1996. *Civil Disabilities of Convicted Felons: A State-by-State Survey.* Washington D.C.: Office of the Pardon Attorney.

Lynch, Mona. 1998. "Waste Managers? New Penology, Crime Fighting, and the Parole Agent Identity." *Law and Society Review.* 32(4):839-869.

Lyons, Donna H. 2000. "'Three Strikes' Sentencing Laws: December 2000." Denver, Colorado: National Conference of State Legislatures.

McCaffrey, Barry. 1998. *Drug Treatment in the Criminal Justice System.* Washington, D.C.: Office of National Drug Control Policy.

McCleary, Richard. 1992. *Dangerous Men: The Sociology of Parole.* New York: Harrow and Heston.

Moore, Gwendolyne S. 2000. July 29 letter from Senator Moore to Governor Thompson regarding the swelling prison population in Wisconsin and the need for alternatives.

Morgan, Terry and Stephen Marrs. 1998. "Redmond, Washington's SMART Partnership for Police and Community Corrections." In Joan Petersilia, ed. *Community Corrections: Probation, Parole, and Intermediate Sanctions.* New York: Oxford University Press. 170-180.

Morse, Wayne. 1939. *U.S. Attorney General's Survey of Release Procedures.* Washington, D.C.: U.S. Department of Justice.

National Conference of State Legislatures. 2001. "Selected, Significant State Crime Enactments in 2000." Denver, Colorado: National Conference of State Legislatures.

National Institute of Corrections. 1995. *Status Report on Parole, 1995.* Washington D.C.: U.S. Department of Justice.

———. 1997. *Status Report on Parole, 1996. Results from an NIC Survey.* Washington D.C.: U.S. Department of Justice.

National Institute of Justice. 2000. *Request for Applications for Reentry Courts Process Evaluation.* Washington, D.C.: National Institute of Justice.

O'Leary, Vincent, ed. 1974. *Parole Administration.* Chicago: Rand McNally Publishing.

Olivares, K., V. Burton, and F. Cullen. 1996. "The Collateral Consequences of a Felony Conviction: A National Study of State Legal Codes 10 Years Later." *Federal Probation.* 60:10-18.

Pan, Philip. 1998. "Maryland Orders Drug Tests for Addicts on Parole." *The Washington Post.* 1.

Parent, Dale. 1993. "Structuring Policies to Address Sanctions for Absconders and Violators." In Edward Rhine, ed. *Reclaiming Offender Accountability: Intermediate Sanctions for Probation and Parole Violators.* Lanham, Maryland: American Correctional Association.

Parent, Dale, Dan Wentworth, Peggy Burke, and Becky Ney. 1994. *Responding to Probation and Parole Violations.* Washington, D.C.: National Institute of Justice.

Petersilia, Joan. 1997. "Probation in America." In Michael Tonty, ed. *Crime and Justice: An Annual Review of Research.* Chicago, Illinois: University of Chicago Press.

———. 1998a. "A Decade of Experimenting with Intermediate Sanctions: What Have We Learned?" In *Perspectives on Crime and Justice.* Washington, D.C.: National Institute of Justice. 79-106.

———. 1998b. "Probation and Parole." In Michael Tonry, ed. *The Oxford Handbook of Criminology.* New York: Oxford University Press.

———. 2000. *When Prisoners Return to the Community: Political, Economic, and Social Consequences.* Washington, D.C.: U.S. Department of Justice, National Institute of Justice.

Petersilia, Joan and Susan Turner. 1993. "Intensive Probation and Parole." In Michael Tonry, ed. *Crime and Justice: An Annual Review of Research.* Chicago, Illinois: University of Chicago Press.

Prendergast, Michael, Douglas Anglin, and Jean Wellisch. 1995. "Treatment for Drug-Abusing Offenders Under Community Supervision." *Federal Probation.* 66.

Reitz, Kevin. 1998. "Sentencing." In Michael Tonry, ed. *The Handbook of Crime and Punishment*. New York: Oxford University Press. 542-562.

Rhine, Edward E. 1996. "Parole Boards." In Marilyn McShane and Frank Williams, eds. *The Encyclopedia of American Prisons*. New York: Garland Publishing, Inc. 342-348.

Rhine, Edward, William Smith, Ronald Jackson, Peggy Burke, and Roger LaBelle. 1991. *Paroling Authorities: Recent History and Current Practice*. Lanham, Maryland: American Correctional Association.

Richards, Stephen C. 1995. *The Structure of Prison Release: An Extended Case Study of Prison Release, Work Release, and Parole*. New York: McGraw-Hill, Inc.

Rothman, David. 1980. *Conscience and Convenience: The Asylum and Its Alternatives in Progressive America*. Boston: Little, Brown.

Rubin, Edward. 1997. *Minimizing Harm as a Goal for Crime Policy in California*. Berkeley, California: California Policy Seminar.

Rudovsky, David, Alvin Bronstein, Edward Koren, and Julie Cade. 1988. *The Rights of Prisoners*. Carbondale, Illinois: Southern Illinois University Press.

Runda, John, Edward Rhine, and Robert Wetter. 1994. *The Practice of Parole Boards*. Lexington, Kentucky: Association of Paroling Authorities, International.

Schlosser, Eric. 1998. *The Prison Industrial Complex. The Atlantic Monthly*. 51-77.

Schwaneberg, Robert. 2001. "Justices Uphold Stricter Parole." *The Star-Ledger* (New Jersey). March 1.

Sechrest, Lee, Susan White, and Elizabeth Brown. 1979. *The Rehabilitation of Criminal Offenders: Problems and Prospects*. Washington, D.C.: National Academy of Sciences.

Sherman, Lawrence, Denise Gottfredson, Doris Mackenzie, John Eck, Peter Reuter, and Shawn Bushway. 1997. *Preventing Crime: What Works, What Doesn't, What's Promising*. College Park, Maryland: University of Maryland.

Simon, Jonathan. 1993. *Poor Discipline: Parole and the Social Control of the Underclass, 1890-1990*. Chicago: The University of Chicago Press.

Smith, Michael and Walter Dickey. 1998. "What If Corrections Were Serious About Public Safety?" *Corrections Management Quarterly*. 2:12-30.

Sundt, Jody, Francis Cullen, Michael Turner, and Brandon Applegate. 1998. "What Will The Public Tolerate?" *Perspectives*. 22:22-26.

Tonn, Ron. 1999. "Turning the Tables: The Safer Foundation's Youth Enterprise Program." *Corrections Today.* 61(1):76, 78.

————. 2001. Telephone conversation with editor, May 11.

Tonry, Michael. 1995. *Malign Neglect: Race, Crime, and Punishment in America.* New York: Oxford University Press.

Travis, Jeremy. 2000. "But They All Come Back: Rethinking Prisoner Reentry." Washington, D.C.: U.S. Department of Justice, National Institute of Justice.

Travis, Jeremy, Amy L. Solomon, and Michelle Waul. 2001. *From Prison to Home: The Dimensions and Consequences of Prisoner Reentry.* Washington, D.C.: Urban Institute Justice Policy Center.

Turner, Susan and Joan Petersilia. 1992. "Focusing on High-Risk Parolees: An Experiment to Reduce Commitment to the Texas Department of Corrections." *The Journal of Research in Crime and Delinquency.* 29:34-61.

————. 1996a. "Work Release in Washington: Effects on Recidivism and Corrections Costs." *The Prison Journal.* 76.

————. 1996b. *Work Release: Recidivism and Corrections Costs in Washington State.* Washington D.C.: National Institute of Justice.

Uggen, Christopher. 2000. "Work as a Turning Point in the Life Course of Criminals: A Duration Model of Age, Employment, and Recidivism." *American Sociological Review.* 67:529-546.

von Hirsch, Andrew. 1976. *Doing Justice: The Choice of Punishments.* New York: Hill and Wang.

von Hirsch, Andrew, and Kathleen Hanrahan. 1979. *The Question of Parole: Retention, Reform, or Abolition?* Cambridge, Massachusetts: Ballinger.

Walker, Samuel. 1998. *A History of American Criminal Justice.* New York: Oxford University Press.

Wilson, James. 1985. *Thinking About Crime.* New York: Basic Books.

Wilson, Rob. 1977. "Release: Should Parole Boards Hold the Key?" *Corrections Magazine.* 47-55.

INDEX

A

Alabama
  civil disabilities of convicted felons, 163
  correctional budgets, 40
alcohol abuse. See substance abuse
Allen, George, 112
American Correctional Association (ACA), 116, 118, 151-152, 170
  parole data source, 124
American Justice Institute, 25
American Probation and Parole Association (APPA), 61-62, 66, 124
anger management, 117
Arizona
  broken windows probation, 66
  caseload funding, 39
  community punishment, 71
  parole supervision in, 116
  prison admissions, 32
  probation utilization, 49
Arkansas, parole supervision in, 116
Association of Paroling Authorities, International (APAI), 124, 151-152, 170
attorney representation and imprisonment related, 28
Augustus, John, 17, 18

B

bail, 17, 23, 28
Beck, Allen, 139
BJS (Bureau of Justice Statistics). *See* Bureau of Justice Statistics (BJS)
black males, 72
Board of Executive Clemency (Arizona), 116
boot camps
  parole conditions, 183
  for probation violaters, 185
  recidivism reductions from, 70

statistics, 34, 69
  Violation of Probation model (Delaware), 7
Boston, broken window probation in, 66
"Break the Cycle" program (Maryland), 156
Brewer v. Morrissey, 159
Brockway, Zebulon, 130-131
broken window probation, 66-67
Bureau of Justice Assistance (BJA), 123
Bureau of Justice Statistics (BJS)
  crime rate surveys, 172
  data provided by, 12
  gender/race of probationers, 47
  imprisonment to probation ratios, 45
  inmate date collection by, 124
  National Corrections Reporting Program, 170
  "National Judicial Reporting Program", 12, 123
  National Pretrial Reporting Program, 59
  parole completion data, 170
  parole/probation agency data, 123
  parole trend information, 124
  parole violation statistics, 169
  parolee characteristics, 123, 146
  probation completion data, 31
  probation follow-up study, 70
  probationers annual survey, 11
  probationers contribution to crime, 59-60
  rearrest rates, 116
  recidivism statistics by status, 60, 60f
  sentencing practices statistics, 45
  Survey of State Prison Inmates, 60

C

California
  adult probation population, 46
  caseloads and contact levels, 35, 35-36
  civil disabilities of convicted felons, 163, 164
  Contra Costs program, 73
  correctional budgets, 40

Note: f=figure or table

V

Vermont, probationer data collection, 11
Violation of Probation centers, Delaware, 6-7
Virginia
civil disabilities of convicted felons, 164
correctional budgets, 40
parole release, 112, 115
parole supervision, 115
parole system adoption, 131
vocational training or programs, 117
von Hirsch, Andrew, 136-137

W

Washington
broken windows probation, 66
community custody in, 116
employment/job training program, 184
parole release, 134
police in probation/parole monitoring, 5-6
probation services funding, 40
probation utilization, 49
work release in, 125
Washington D.C.
civil disabilities of convicted felons, 164
drug courts in, 4
parole release (discretionary), 112
parole supervision statistics, 145
truth-in-sentencing laws, 112
West Virginia, electronic monitoring in, 40
What Works, 117-118
Wilson, James Q., 5, 136
Wisconsin
intermediate sanctions programs (ISPs), 70
neighborhood parole, 186
women probationers, 47
Woodward, Bill, 115
work training for parolees, 125

ABOUT THE AUTHOR

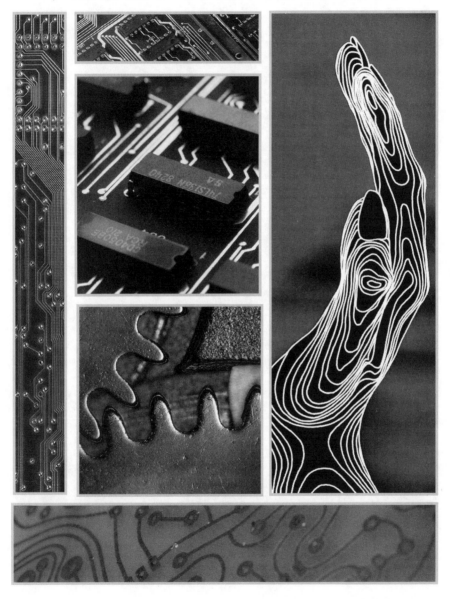

Joan Petersilia, Ph.D., is a professor of criminology, law and society in the School of Social Ecology, University of California, Irvine. Prior to joining the University, she was the director of the criminal justice program at RAND. She has directed major studies in policing, sentencing, career criminals, parole, juvenile justice, corrections, and racial discrimination. Dr. Petersilia's current work focuses on probation, parole, intermediate sanctions, and prisoner reentry.

Dr. Petersilia has served as president of both the American Society of Criminology and of the Association of Criminal Justice Research in California. She is an elected fellow of the American Society of Criminology, and received its Vollmer Award for her overall contributions to crime and public policy.

She also has received awards from the American Probation and Parole Association, and the California Probation, Parole, and Corrections Association for her dedication to community corrections. She is currently the vice chair of the National Research Council's Committee on Law and Justice, and is an adviser to several organizations, including the Los Angeles County Sheriff's Department, the Ventura County Probation Department, the Los Angeles County Probation Department, the National Institute of Justice, the California Policy Seminar, the Urban Institute, and RAND.

Her most recent books are *Crime: Public Policies for Crime Control* with James Q. Wilson (2002); *Crime Victims with Developmental Disabilities* (2001); *Prisons: A Review of Research* (1999); *Prisons*, edited with Michael Tonry (1999); *Criminal Justice Policy* (1998); *Community Corrections* (1998); and *Crime*, edited with James Q. Wilson (1995). She is the author of more than 100 chapters and articles, including "Reentry Reconsidered: A New Look at an Old Question," (2001);

"Doing Justice? Criminal Offenders with Developmental Disabilities" (2001); "American Prisons at the Beginning of the Twenty-First Century" (1999); "Parole and Prisoner Reentry" (1999); "Justice for All? Offenders with Mental Retardation and Corrections" (1998); "Probation in America" (1997); "A Crime Control Rationale for Reinvesting in Community Corrections" (1995); "Twenty-five Years of NIJ and Its Research Program" (1994); "Debating Crime and Punishment in California"(1994); "Intensive Probation and Parole" (1993); "Smart Sentencing: the Emergence of Intermediate Sanctions" (1992); "Expanding Options for Criminal Sentencing" (1987); "Police Performance and Case Attrition" (1987); "The Influence of Criminal Justice Research" (1987); "Prison vs. Probation in California" (1986); "Granting Felons Probation" (1985); and "Racial Disparities in the Criminal Justice System" (1983).

Dr. Petersilia has a BA (1972) in sociology from Loyola University of Los Angeles, an MA (1974) in sociology from Ohio State University, and a Ph.D. (1990) in criminology, law and society, from the University of California, Irvine.